LUTON CORPORATION TRANSPORT

LUTON
CORPORATION
TRANSPORT

PETER ROSE

The
History
Press

First published 2009

The History Press
The Mill, Brimscombe Port
Stroud, Gloucestershire, GL5 2QG
www.thehistorypress.co.uk

British Library Cataloguing in Publication Data.
A catalogue record for this book is available from the British Library.

ISBN 978 0 7524 4913 5

Typesetting and origination by The History Press
Printed in Great Britain

CONTENTS

PREFACE

My interest in buses goes back to my early childhood. For some reason the red buses were a particular fascination to me. When I conceived the idea of writing this book I was unaware of any publication about Luton Corporation Transport (LCT), and therefore began research in 1991 with the intention of gathering information for an informal publication.

There are, of course, other books available which include information about this subject, but this book is as much for my own satisfaction as that of any interested reader.

I have provided some transport background on the Luton area prior to the Corporation buses, including, with the invaluable help of others, a brief history of the trams. By doing so I hope that I have given a comprehensive backcloth to the emergence of the LCT Transport undertaking. My research has also given me an insight into some of the day-to-day problems that were encountered, which may very well be similar to many other municipal bus undertakings during the period covered.

A debt of gratitude is owed to all those people who have helped me in gathering information. Various organisations and publications have also provided me with the opportunity to verify facts. In instances where historical facts are uncertain or information that has been derived from varying sources conflict, I have endeavoured to make this clear. Lastly, I cannot claim to be an expert on the subject, and offer my apologies in advance to any reader who may feel they disagree with any of the content.

Peter Rose
Letchworth, 2009

ABOUT THE AUTHOR

Born in Bedford in 1944, Peter Rose's family moved to the Stopsley area of Luton in 1946, at that time a village to the north-east of Luton. As a child he took a keen interest in the local buses. He was educated in Luton and commenced a career with Barclays Bank, Luton, in 1960, taking advantage of an early retirement opportunity from management in 1995. He now lives with his wife in Letchworth, where he has lived since 1972, and has interests in photography, local history, veteran scooters, caravanning and fell walking.

PUBLIC TRANSPORT BEFORE TRAMS

Early public transport existed in the Luton area long before the arrival of trams, although these only ran to other population centres, rather than on a local basis.

Life in Luton in the eighteenth century depended much upon owning a horse. At that time Luton was not a coaching town. Roads to and from the town were not good. Most horse-drawn coaches used the routes either along the Great North Road (A1) or Watling Street (A5).

To illustrate the difficulties of travel at that time, it took some twelve hours to reach London by coach from Luton. In 1794 the *Ampthill Flyer* began a twice-weekly service to London, through Luton. The journey to Luton took three and a half hours, arriving in time for the evening meal, then a further twelve hours to London the following day. In 1810 the travel time to London was reputedly reduced to nine hours, and, as roads improved, by 1836 this had been reduced to four and a half hours.

Later the *Luton Times* coach ran to St Albans, and then via Watling Street to London, taking four hours. Another, called the *Industry Omnibus*, went to Wheathampstead, Hatfield, and along the Great North Road. Following some road improvements, an alternative Ampthil–Manchester coach called *Peveril of the Peak* eventually changed its route to go through Luton instead of Dunstable. Probably the last local horse-drawn coach, as opposed to horse-drawn omnibus, to run in 1858, this took train passengers to Watford, prior to the opening of the Great Northern line at Luton.

The Dunstable branch line, which had been built in 1848, took passengers to Leighton Buzzard, and then to Euston. A horse-drawn coach also ran from Dunstable Station to Luton.

The Great Northern branch line from Hatfield, via Welwyn, and then Luton to Dunstable, was completed in 1858. The Midland line, which ran from St Pancras, was not completed until 1868, and passed through Luton to Bedford and beyond. Until 1858 Luton had been acknowledged as the largest town in England without a railway.

The first discernible 'bus services' in the Luton area were provided by Samuel Hayden, introduced around 1860. This was a horse-drawn service which followed two known routes. One travelled between Hitchin and Luton on Tuesdays and Saturdays, both market days, and the other ran from Luton to Hemel Hempstead, each endeavouring to keep to a timetable. Hitchin Station had opened in 1851, and provided another direct main line link with Kings Cross on the Great Northern line.

By the turn of the century there were also a few operators who emerged between Luton and the villages around the town. The Hitchin bus served Stopsley, whilst separate services ran to Leagrave and Limbury. There were others that operated on a trial basis, but these did not last long. There also remained a good many carriages, operating like taxis.

It is understood that in 1901 a horse bus travelled the Leagrave Road in Luton, owned by Mr Jabez 'Topper' Cain of Lilley. The bus was garaged at Holly Tree Farm, Leagrave. Also, a Mr James Pollard may have operated on this road. Mr Cain's horses were requisitioned by the army in August 1914, and the bus was withdrawn and succeeded by a laundaulette owned by William Burnage.

In September 1905 a local 'Motorbus' service commenced operating between Luton Town Square and the newly opened Wardown Park. This was provided by B.E. Barrett and was probably on a one-month trial basis. In 1906 Commer Cars Ltd offered a similar service.

1. Believed to be Mr Cain's horse bus outside the Sugar Loaf at Leagrave.

2. Believed to be Mr Cain's horse bus.

Around mid-1906 an attempt was made to link Dunstable and Luton by the Herts & Beds Omnibus syndicate. Even though this scheme had been supported by the London Motor Omnibus Co. of London (Vanguard) nothing came of the idea. In 1907 a proposal to link Toddington, Dunstable and Luton on a circular route, to be run by a Clarkson Steam bus, was also abandoned.

In both a book by John Cummings, published by the London Historical Research Group, and in the Omnibus Society Historical Research Group publication, *Public Motor Transport in Bedfordshire 1899–1919*, you can find a full account of motorbuses in the Luton area during this period.

TRAM DAYS
1908–1932

To begin to relate the history of a local bus undertaking without a few words about the tram era that preceded buses would be unworthy of any author.

In 1898 Luton Borough Council took the decision to build a power station. At the same time consideration was given to operating a tramcar system, but probably due to cost this idea was not pursued. In 1901 the privately funded Luton, Dunstable & District Light Railway Co. had endeavoured to commence a tramway connecting Luton and Houghton Regis, via Dunstable. They were unsuccessful due to much local opposition. The proposal was revived as Luton & District Tramways in 1904, with some lines advocated within Luton, omitting the Dunstable–Houghton Regis section. With continued opposition from Luton Borough Council, the Bill failed.

The council opposed the Bill because it had been considering use of its own power station, to be opened on 10 July 1901 by Lord Kelvin, an electrical pioneer. The borough council had been studying various schemes of its own for a tramcar since early 1901, as, like many other municipalities, they desired to own their own system. They were likely driven to positive action in November 1904, prompted by the efforts of those behind the Bill who they had opposed earlier that year. Presented by the borough council, an Act of Parliament was passed, Luton Corporation Tramways Order Confirmation (No.2) Act 1905, whereby the council was given the necessary authority to operate tramcars. After favourable route proposals the council advertised for both a contractor and operator. They contracted a London-based company, J.G. White & Co., who were experienced in construction, but whose operating experience was mainly in the Empire and South America. George Balfour and Andrew Beatty were the commercial manager and secretary, respectively, of J.G. White & Co. Ltd, which was itself the British subsidiary of an American tramway company. There were a number of objections, principally from retailers who felt the streets were too narrow, and that there would be insufficient unloading space for horse-drawn vehicles. Thought was given to a narrower gauge of 3ft 6in, but the standard 4ft 8½in was eventually accepted on safety grounds.

It took five months to complete the work, commencing 7 October 1907 and finishing in February 1908. Quite an achievement, during what had been a difficult winter. The actual route length was 5.25 miles, equal to 6.25 miles of single track. There were no additions to the system in subsequent years.

With the system complete the trials, which occurred after midnight on 13 February, were quite a local spectacle. Crowds were large despite the fact that the date of the trials should have been a secret. A local paper, the *Luton Times*, described the sight of an illuminated electric tramcar gliding along the street as an 'unqualified success'. This was despite one of the cars running off the end of the powered overhead on a corner and everyone having to alight to push it, if only a few yards!

Following inspection by the Board of Trade on 18 February, speed limits were set at a maximum of 12mph in New Bedford Road, Park Street, and part of Dunstable Road, with 4mph on all curves,

3. Trams following delivery at the Park Street depot, February 1908.

4. Park Street tram depot, pictured after buses were introduced.

points and downhill runs. Otherwise the limit was 8mph. Difficulties arose with regard the opening ceremony. It had been hoped that Lloyd George, president of the Board of Trade, would preside over the proceedings, but he was unavailable. Others who were approached declined, knowing that they were not first choice. The local Liberal MP, T.G. Ashton, eventually performed the ceremony, despite reputedly having had a heavy cold, on what was a bitterly cold day. Tramcars 1, 2 and 3 were decorated in red, white and blue bunting. These travelled all three routes and concluded at the Town Hall where there were speeches and toasts.

The new depot was built in Park Street which, in later years, was to become the bus depot. The routes were as shown below (no route numbers were carried, only the names of their destinations):

i) Park Street (Bailey Street – depot entrance at junction with Bailey Street) authorised to New Trapps Lane (later to become Cutenhoe Road, but not built beyond depot) via George Street, Manchester Street, Mill Street, Midland Road, High Town Road, Hitchin Road, terminating at Round Green outside the Shepherd & Flock. This was reputedly a favourite place for refreshment for the drivers, who were often accused of taking a little too much. Although no doubt there was some truth in this, it is said that many simply used the toilets! See (ii) below for changes to route in 1914.

ii) Town Hall, Upper George Street, Dunstable Road, terminating at Kingsway terminus at the Steam Laundry. The destination carried was Dunstable Road. Around April 1914 the route was extended from the Town Hall to Bailey Street, while the Round Green route above was curtailed to terminate at the Town Hall.

iii) London Road (Tennyson Road junction), Ashton Road, Hibbert Street, Chapel Street, George Street, Manchester Street, New Bedford Road, terminating at Wardown Park Lodge (later Bath Road). Curtailed at Lansdowne Road during winter until 1914 then at all times until summer 1919. This was a lightly loaded route since it was a short level walk to town; hence the later introduction of single-deck car No.13 (see later). Driver was paid an extra ¼d per hour.

The system had originally been leased to J.G. White & Co. Ltd to operate on behalf of the corporation for five years. Rumours of a transfer of the lease had been rife for a while: the council debated the issue on 4 May 1909, and eventually agreed to the surrender of the lease to Balfour Beatty and Co. Ltd – a newly formed company, established in January 1909 to take over both Luton and Dartford tramways from J.G. White & Co. Ltd. This new leasing arrangement lasted from May 1909 until after J.G. White Ltd withdrew from the UK market on 21 February 1923, when the corporation took over the system. At the time they took over the system, in 1909, Balfour Beatty & Co. Ltd had inaugurated a feeder bus from Leagrave, which ran until 1912 (see chapter 3). The vehicle proved unreliable. An idea in late 1910 to link the Wardown tram terminus with Leagrave via a cross-country light railway was abandoned after Luton Borough Council refused to agree to a connection at Wardown. There were also cost considerations.

The trams had begun operation on 21 February 1908. The livery was green and white with gold lining. All double-deck cars 1–12 had 'Luton Corporation Tramways' in gold letters along the sides, together with the borough coat of arms. The single-deck car, No.13, purchased later, only had room for 'Corporation Tramways' due to the short length of the saloon.

The tramcars were double-deck, open top, and seated fifty-four; twenty-two inside, eleven along each side facing inwards, thirty-two on top facing forwards on reversible 'garden' seats. Two four-pole, 30hp, series wound, four-wheel units called trucks powered each tramcar. Bogies were of a short wheelbase. Trucks on 1–12 were Brill type, designated 21EM, and built by Mountain & Gibson, Bury Lancs., presumably under licence. The bodies were built by United Electric Tramcar of Preston, with a 6ft wheelbase; and a length of 27ft 6in for the cars. Units purchased were all double-deck open tops. 1, 2, 4 and 5 were later fitted with covered tops by Brush in 1929. No.8 was severely damaged in an accident at the junction of Midland Road and Old Bedford Road on 28 December 1916, and was out of service for eighteen months. The only addition to the fleet was No.13, purchased from Glasgow Corporation. Originally one of a series of double-deck horse trams built between 1894 and 1898, it had been converted to an electric car and fitted with Brill 21E truck with two 30hp motors by Westlinghouse 49B, and type 210 Westlinghouse controllers. Glasgow Corporation had used it as a parcels car for about six months, then as a ticket box car. The Glasgow car No.118 was purchased and cut down to single-deck with a front exit by Luton in 1923. At least twenty-five years old, this unit probably seated eleven each side, twenty-two in all. It was used mainly on the quieter Wardown route.

5. LCT motormen and staff pictured outside the depot.

Motormen (drivers) were initially paid 5*d* an hour and conductors 4½*d* per hour. The Tramway Committee investigated wages in 1909 and found them reasonable compared with other systems. There were strikes for increased wages in August 1918. The men claimed for 6*d* per hour, but settled for 5½*d* or 5*d*. The work was organised in shifts: 6–2, 2–10 or 11. Drivers would have to rise at 4 a.m. to walk the several miles necessary to reach the depot by 6 a.m. Drivers wore raincoats and boots as there were no windscreens on the trams. No seat was provided for the driver either. Picture the poor fellow on a wet day, with the rain running into his boots! Many drivers spoke of their cars being struck by lightning, which was considered an occupational hazard! One described how the electric meter situated at the bulkhead, above the passenger entrance, melted down an inspector's neck during one such incident at Kingsway. Facilities were non-existent; there was no canteen, and no sandwiches were eaten on the platform at the end of a run. If he happened to pass home en route perhaps a hot soup would be handed to the driver by his wife. Kindly townsfolk would sometimes send out a servant with tea, particularly Mrs Blunham, wife of the Revd Blunham, Vicar of St Paul's, who lived on London Road. She was also known to pay 6*d* for a 1*d* fare. Extra money was sometimes made by stopping especially for a well-known citizen, outside his house, to save him the walk to a stop. Mr Wiseman of London Road was one such person.

The accounts for the first full year's operation showed a loss of £1,000. Trams had carried 2,131,635 passengers and had travelled 279,102 miles. This meant that the population had been carried fifty times over during the year. The people of the town had been told that the tramways would only be profitable if they carried thirty-three times over. It was then revealed that this figure had related to a smaller scheme! At this time Dunstable Road services were altered to start from Park Square so they could provide a service every ten minutes, instead of the previous fifteen minutes' interval. Round Green cars continued to work from the depot and some consideration was given to the issue of transfer tickets for a change of car at the Town Hall. A letter in the *Luton Reporter* of 15 April 1909 again raised the question of obtaining workmen's tickets on the cars. The writer suggested that the same timed car could be a workmen's service on some days, if not on others. He also enquired as to why women workers were not treated in the byelaws as workmen. Early discrimination!

Balfour Beatty were not satisfied with the system and made no secret of their wish to terminate the operating lease, but it was not until February 1923 that the corporation took over the operation of the system.

Although the system remained profitable and the number of passengers continued to grow, by 1929 the impact of local motorbus transport services, particularly by covered-top buses from

6. George Street, Luton, in 1930, showing both open-topped and roofed trams.

7. Single-deck tram car No. 13, a converted horse-drawn tram bought second-hand from Glasgow. This was a one-man-operated tram.

National, was being felt. The need to renew all tracks would (it was envisaged) arise after 1930. The question of tram replacement was considered. Trams ceased operation on 16 April 1932. The last tram, No.7, ran from Round Green to the depot, arriving around 11.30 on a Saturday night, in pouring rain. Buses had gradually replaced trams since 1 March 1932. Some tramlines were torn up and the drivers trained to drive the new Daimler buses. Some tramlines remained, but certainly those in George Street were taken up in 1932. When road improvements within Luton took place in 1969 some line was found in Upper George Street. Similarly, in 1970, junction improvements at Mill Street and New Bedford Road revealed track left under the tarmac. It is also believed that track also remains under High Town Road. Three traction poles are erected outside Wardown Museum, in use as lampposts.

The single-deck tram, No.13, was the first to be towed into the Dust Destructor Works drive, by Powdrills traction engine. The trams stood idle for nearly a year awaiting a buyer. Some interest was shown by Bexley Corporation but came to nothing. Local metal dealer Thomas Oakley of Beechwood Road, Luton, showed a little interest but declined to make an offer. Eventually the single-decker No.13 was sold for conversion to a chicken house at Round Green, Luton. The twelve double-deck trams were sold to the national scrap dealer Thos. W. Ward of Silvertown. Several bodies were resold locally, and dismantled at the Dust Destructor Works depot. There were newspaper reports of a double-decker being sold to a W.H. Bowden, but it is thought that this was the No.13 mentioned earlier. However, only two are known to have survived: No.2 was sited in Streatley, Beds, but was burnt out in 1960, and No.6 was cut down by Messrs Jones Cotton & Co. at their Tavistock Street Dunstable engineering works, and used as an office. This was still in use in 1970, but disappeared shortly afterwards. During 1988 I was fortunate enough to trace No.6, then in use as a greenhouse on a farm at Newton Purcell in Oxfordshire. Luton Museum subsequently transported this unit to its new home at Stockwood Park Museum, for eventual restoration as a tribute to a lost era.

A full account of Luton's trams can be found in the book by Colin Brown, published by the Irwell Press, entitled *Luton Trams: The Story of a Small System 1908–1932*.

3

EARLY BUSES
1908–1933

On 14 August 1909, following requests from the Limbury and Leagrave Local Council, and to prove viability of a tramway to Leagrave, Balfour Beatty & Co. augmented the tram service from Luton by establishing a bus service from the junction at Leagrave and Dunstable Road to the Sugar Loaf at Leagrave. This alternative was seen as less expensive than extending the system. The vehicle used had solid tyres and was a chain-driven, eighteen-seat, 30/32hp Commer bus with the registration LM 8152, leased from Commercial Car Hirers Ltd.

Initially a half-hourly service was provided, but this was soon reduced to hourly due to an inability to maintain the original schedule. Erratic connections with the tram service caused much annoyance.

The operation was not viable and the bus kept getting stuck in mud on poor roads. Due to unreliability the Balfour Beatty & Co. service ceased in November 1912. Eventually, at the request of Leagrave Parish Council, the bus service was taken over by Road Motors on 14 November of that year. Road Motors themselves withdrew after 30 June 1913, as the operation remained unprofitable. The first and last journeys originated at Luton Town Hall, due, no doubt, to the fact that their vehicles were kept in the yard at the Horse & Jockey in Manchester Street, opposite the Town Hall.

Another bus service connecting the trams commenced on 31 October 1910. This was operated by the Dunstable Road Car Co. and commenced from Dunstable at the Saracen's Head, initially to connect with the Luton Trams at their Kingsway terminus on Dunstable Road. Despite attempts to gain Luton Watch Committee approval, permission was withheld for a through service to George Street, Luton, except on Sundays. The service didn't last long. Initially it ran daily, but by April 1911 it only ran three days a week, reverting to daily by June, and was discontinued at the end of 1911. Local timetables quoted the service as 'subject to serious/continual alterations', possibly due to a lack of staff or an erratic vehicle/s.

Continued efforts to operate a through service to the centre of Luton on weekdays were thwarted by LCT, using the excuse of narrow streets, so safeguarding the trams. More information about buses in the Dunstable and Luton area can be found in *Forgotten Bus Operations* by J.M. Cummings, published by the London Historical Research Group.

This chapter now traces the earlier bus operators in the Luton area, who eventually developed to form the principle three stage operators, namely London Transport, Eastern National (later transferred to United Counties) and LCT. To best illustrate the history, three groups of businesses are identified, which led to the formation of the above operators. Natural development of private operators during the period of the trams was inevitable, as the trams could obviously only offer a geographically restricted service.

8. Balfour Beatty's Luton–Leagrave bus.

GROUP 1

Road Motors Ltd, National, Eastern National, then United Counties:

Thomas J. Attree started Luton's first successful motorbus service in May 1912 when his London-registered company Road Motors Ltd introduced a Luton–Hitchin–Letchworth bus service. Although other services to Leagrave, Dunstable and Clophill were introduced shortly afterwards, only the Letchworth service was in operation by the end of the First World War, by which time the company's depot and registered office was in Langley Street, Luton. Post-war expansion saw the introduction of bus services between Letchworth and Norton, Leagrave, Dunstable, St Albans, Hertford, Markyate, Wheathampstead, Toddington, Woburn, Sundon, Redbourn, Houghton Regis, Caddington, Limbury, Dallow Road and Stopsley, together with an outpost at Weymouth operating a local service. In addition to the Langley Street premises vehicles were out-stationed at St Albans during 1921, and at Letchworth at Norton. Additional garage premises were added at Radipole (Weymouth) and Toddington by the time the business was sold to the National Omnibus & Transport Co. (NO & TC) in April 1925.

The National Steam Car Co. had operated Clarkson steam buses in London and Essex since 1909, but wartime maintenance difficulties had brought about a need to change the fleet to motorbus operation in 1919. An agreement with the London & General Omnibus Co. (LGOC) saw the replacement of the London operations with premises in Bedford, which had been unused by LGOC since November 1914. Motorbus operations spread quickly throughout Bedfordshire, the company's title from February 1920 becoming the NO & TC. The Borough Watch Committee delayed entry into central Luton, but eventually a service from Leighton Buzzard started in April 1920. The company was also actively expanding in the West of England at this time. An agreement was reached with LGOC in summer 1921 for National to operate services in Hertfordshire using vehicles supplied by LGOC from premises financed by the London operator. Shortly afterwards another agreement was concluded with Road Motors which included clauses concerning non-competitive expansion in the Luton area. After acquisition by NO & TC of Road Motors' business in April 1925, the area covered by the LGOC agreement was extended northwards from St Albans to cover the area south of Luton, to be effective from early 1927. A new garage in Castle Street, Luton, opened in 1927 and housed LGOC National vehicles in red livery for services southwards, and green-liveried National vehicles for other services. In March 1929 National acquired Ideal Motor Coaches Ltd of Dunstable, who operated from Dunstable to Edlesborough.

During 1929, agreement was reached between National, the four main-line railway companies, Thomas Tilling Ltd (already part owners of National) and the British Electric Traction group for the company's ownership to be passed jointly to these latter bodies. During 1930 the Bedfordshire area, together with Essex, became the Eastern National Omnibus Co. (ENOC) with part ownership

9. Road Motors No.35, reg. NM 4216, at Dallow Road, Luton.

by the LMS and LNER railway companies; although for the time being the operations covered by the LGOC agreement remained under direct 'National' operation. Toward the end of 1930 Eastern National prepared an offer of £64,000 to acquire Luton's trams (see chapter 4). Eventually, control of Eastern National passed to the Tilling Group and voluntarily nationalised in August 1948. Rationalisation of company areas within the state-owned sector resulted in the Bedfordshire area being transferred from Eastern National to the Northampton-based United Counties Omnibus Co. (UC) in May 1952.

GROUP 2

London Transport and its Predecessors

The London Passenger Transport Act established London Transport from 1933 as the main provider of local transport (apart from the mainline railways) within Greater London and part of the surrounding Home Counties, and as territorial bus operator for a further section of the Home Counties which included the area south of Luton. As such, the Board acquired the buses and operations run by National under agreement to the LGOC, which had been temporarily maintained by a new company, London General Country Services Ltd, from March 1932 until July 1933.

London Transport also acquired the Luton-based business of Harry Hill's Strawhatter Motor Coaches. This had started as a small private-hire venture in 1923, by B.E. Barrett of Langley Street Garage, but had expanded substantially from 1927 onwards with the introduction of a Luton–London daily coach service. The business passed to Harry Hill in 1931. Competition on the Luton–London express service was fierce, with Priest's Imperial Services, Allan Smith's Imperial Luton–Bedford Services Ltd, Parrott's Beech Hill Safety Coach and Birch Bros. All tried, but withdrew during 1928, leaving only 'Strawhatter' and 'Venture of Hendon' on the service. The introduction by Green Line Coaches Ltd (associated with LGOC) of an express service from Harpenden to London brought more competition from September 1930. Strawhatter acquired the Venture operations on the Luton–London service in January 1933, but subsequently accepted a generous acquisition bid from London Transport. The business was acquired on 1 February 1934, together with Strawhatter's garage at Park Street West, which became London Transport's garage in Luton, enabling vehicles to be removed from the Eastern National premises in Castle Street. Strawhatter's seasonal coastal express services subsequently passed to Eastern National, whilst a small road haulage operation later passed to Pickford's.

GROUP 3

Bluebird Services, XL Motor Services, Union Jack, A.F. England and Luton Corporation

At the turn of the century, the England family ran the main bakery in Dunstable, based in High Street South, and owned land adjacent to these premises in the area now around Britain Street and Lovers Walk. The property then included open land, nurseries and tennis courts. There were seven children in the family; five girls and two boys. The elder boy, Bert, had a flair for engineering and was later well known for his cycle business in the town. The younger brother, Arthur, who preferred to be known by his middle name, Fred, was renowned for his business acumen. Fred's first venture into managing his own business started in March 1921 when he began running a Ford van on delivery works from the family property. He fitted fourteen seats in it for occasional passenger private hire. A further Ford vehicle, this time a purpose-built coach, was added in 1923.

Fred's venture into bus work did not start until April 1927, with a small fleet of new, small capacity Ford and Laffley vehicles in blue (later two tone blue and white) livery forming XL Service. Recognising the inadequacy of National's bus services to Houghton Regis, he introduced a frequent Luton–Houghton Regis–Dunstable bus service, the Dunstable terminus at Great Northern Road also serving the England family property and encouraging development. Off-peak journeys were extended to Hockliffe and Leighton Buzzard, competing with National's service 18, with services to Wing, Ivinghoe and Tring (on market days only) added during 1929–30. Larger Dennis vehicles replaced the small Laffleys, culminating with a brand new fifty-seat double-deck Dennis Lance in December 1931.

In spring 1931, Fred England gained control of the Union Jack (Luton) Omnibus Co. Ltd. This business had originated as a venture by Hubert Witherington, of the Griffin Hotel at Toddington, in June 1928, which concentrated on providing works transport from the villages around Toddington into Vauxhall Works at Luton, for which the National's bus services were poorly timed and expensive. It appears that a lunchtime facility was also provided locally in Luton to take Vauxhall workers home to and from New Town Street area, and possibly the Old Bedford Road area as well. Unfortunately, Witherington was caught carrying local passengers illegally along Leagrave Road, Luton. He was prosecuted and his business threatened with closure. Witherington operated in a true pirate fashion, often flaunting licensing laws.

In September 1928 two Luton publicans, Charles Strapps of The Rabbit on Old Bedford Road and Amos Barber of The Robin Hood on New Town Street, offered to buy the Witherington bus business in conjunction with Messrs Williams & Webb, owners of the Excelsior garage in Albert Road, Luton, adjacent to The Robin Hood. They formed the Union Jack (Luton) Omnibus Co. Ltd. Control of the Witherington business passed to the new company in November 1928. Details of fleet and operations are vague: it was claimed that some twelve services operated at the time of transfer. By spring 1931 there was just one roadworthy vehicle kept at the Excelsior garage. Buses operated between Vauxhall Works and Leighton Buzzard on weekdays, and one off-peak between Luton and Studham (also possibly some lunchtime contract work from Vauxhall). It is unclear how Fred England gained control of this moribund business, but he agreed with the newly established Traffic Commissioners to withdraw the Luton–Studham service in exchange for a share of the Luton–Whipsnade Zoo bus service, following the zoo's opening in May 1931. The registered office and operating base was moved to England's Dunstable premises and a new Dennis was painted in the Union Jack livery.

In early 1932, Fred England became involved with H.J. Hinds & Co.'s Bluebird Services. This Luton-based business had a similar background to England's XL Service. Herbert Hinds, whose family owned property off Old Bedford Road in Luton, started private hire work using charabancs in about 1919, based initially in High Town Road, Luton. Painted blue, they were titled 'Bluebirds'. Hinds, in conjunction with his first partner, Thorogood, formed a limited company, H.J. Hinds & Co. The business expanded, although fleet records are scant, with Thorogood being replaced as a partner by Earnest Savage, and a purpose-built depot being established at Wardown garage in New Bedford Road – in later years the site of a filling station.

The Bluebird coach fleet and original depot were destroyed by fire around January 1927. The replacement fleet would concentrate on bus work during the week, with private hire work on

10. Bluebird Motors, reg. BM8480, on private hire pictured in Inkerman Street, Luton.

Sundays. Three small fourteen-seat buses started operations during June/July 1927 on short routes from Bridge Street, Luton, to Stockingstone Road, and to Biscot Mill via Cromwell Hill, as well as to Leagrave via Biscot Road, the latter two in competition with National's services. Other small vehicles joined the fleet, with a larger Dennis entering service in 1930. New services started to Streatley, Barton, Hexton and Pegsdon, to Leagrave, Dunstable and Whipsnade Zoo, and to Colin Road. By late 1931 the small-capacity vehicles were unable to cope with the growing traffic due to expansion around Biscot Mill and the 'Saints' area. The company had no finance to buy larger vehicles.

A new company, Hinds & Savage Ltd, was formed with additional capital provided by Fred England, but by June 1932 the Bluebird business was acquired completely by the Union Jack (Luton) Omnibus Co. Ltd. Under new ownership, the Bluebird fleet was largely replaced by higher-capacity single-deck Dennis buses, mostly acquired second-hand, but it was apparent that LCT was by now interested in its acquisition.

However, Fred England was unwilling to discuss a 'piece meal' disposal of his bus business. Instead, they would have to bid for his entire bus operation, including leases on properties at Bridge Street, Luton, the Bluebird enquiry office, New Bedford Road, Luton, the Bluebird garage and Britain Street, Dunstable, the XL premises which were leased from the England family anyway! Although the deal was finalised in October 1932 for £21,000, the Traffic Commissioners were unable to agree which licences should be transferred until early 1933, so the deal only took effect from 23 March 1933.

Under the terms of the LCT deal, Fred England retained the title of the Union Jack (Luton) Omnibus Co. Ltd registered at Lovers Walk, Dunstable, but no vehicles or operations.

Although outside the direct scope of this book, it is worth completing the story of Fred England's involvement with bus operations. Whilst awaiting the transfer of his earlier bus businesses to LCT (and the £21,000 payment) Fred was already actively reinvesting the anticipated capital, recognising the 'nuisance value' of small bus operators to the large territorial operators now being established. In early 1933, he was negotiating with two other small bus businesses, based in Bedford and Luton, over a possible acquisition.

The Carding family had established a coach and bus business in Kempston, Bedford, in March 1927, operated by Albert Carding and his two sons, Percy and R.A. Carding. The bus operations were centred mainly on the Bedford–Kempston local service, on which they competed with National and many other smaller operators, trading under the name Wonder Bus, although a Bedford–Cranfield service was operated in competition with National for a while. R.A. Carding became involved with Herbert Clench's ill-fated 'Dreadnought Bus Service' during 1928–30, but when that business collapsed he returned to the family business, operating Dreadnought's Midland Road–Stanley Street, Bedford, town service and their share of the Bedford–Harrold service. Despite the formation of a limited company under the title Swallow Bus & Coach Co. Ltd, the Carding business remained short of capital. By 1932, they were the only small operator left on the Bedford–Kempston service, on which they were running small-capacity ageing coaches alongside large new double-deck vehicles operated by Eastern National. Fred England's offer involved only the acquisition of the Bedford local services and one small twenty-seat vehicle. Swallow Bus & Coach Co. Ltd would continue their coach operations from Kempston, together with their share of the Harrold Country bus service (which was eventually sold to Birch Bros. Ltd in 1938).

Union Jack (Luton) Omnibus Co. Ltd took over Carding's share of the Bedford local services in March 1933, initially using demonstration vehicles (an Albion and a Thornycroft double-deck, and an Albion and two Maudslay large-capacity single-deck buses) to maintain the Bedford services until finance from the LCT deal was available to purchase these vehicles. The vehicles were kept in the yard of the Simplex Works in Elstow Road, Bedford, within sight of the Eastern National premises. The vehicles were even painted in a two tone green and cream livery similar to that used by their much larger rival. Other second-hand vehicles were added to the fleet, mainly Dennis vehicles, including several small twenty-seat buses bought back from LCT.

Meanwhile, Fred England had also been active in the Luton area, for on 27 March 1933, just a few days after the disposal of his earlier Luton area bus operations to LCT, his Union Jack (Luton) Omnibus Co. Ltd acquired the 'Renown Motors' bus business of the Lamb Bros. of Langley Road, Luton. Sidney and H. Lamb had both worked for Road Motors Ltd, and then National, but had left the latter's employment in the summer of 1927 to set up their own business, with two vehicles operating a daily bus service, in competition with National, between Luton and Markyate, continuing to Flamstead. Although records are scant, they never owned more than two vehicles at a time, but provided an intensive timetable, targeting in particular peak-hour travellers to and from Luton's factories. In their early days of operation the Lamb Bros. had repeatedly failed to gain permission from the Luton Watch Committee to increase their fleet size or introduce other services. With the former National service to Markyate likely to pass to the new London Passenger Transport Board (LPTB) in July 1933, the 'Renown' operation would become a serious competitor to the London Transport service – another instance of an under-funded bus operation likely to become a thorn in the side of a much bigger operator! Union Jack acquired the operations in March 1933, with just one vehicle, and immediately boosted the fleet with second-hand Dennis buses operating from the England family premises in Britain Street, Dunstable. Once again the adopted livery of dark green and white showed a remarkable resemblance to that later adopted as London Transport's country bus livery!

Despite acquisition overtures from both Eastern National and London Transport for their respective parts of the Union Jack business, Fred England again refused to consider splitting the business, which would only be available for sale in total. Whilst the two major operators agreed amongst themselves to a formula for a joint acquisition, valuing the business at about £8,000 in 1934, little progress was made. New contract and excursion work was added, and the Union Jack fleet at Dunstable and Bedford grew to over fifteen vehicles. In July 1935 the one bus business of Thomas Allen of Kempston was acquired for £1,700, together with his share of the Bedford–Kimbolton–St Neots service, operated in coordination with Eastern National. Thomas Allen had been a driver with the ill-fated Dreadnought bus service in the late twenties and took over this bus service with one vehicle when Dreadnought collapsed in 1930. His small twenty-seat Bedford was often inadequate for the bus service and hired vehicles were often used for duplicates.

Eventually, it was Eastern National who opened acquisition talks with Fred England. It was agreed that Tilling Co. acquire the entire Union Jack business, with London Transport paying a pro-rata proportion for the Luton–Flamstead service after three months' operation by Eastern National, in which the relative values would be assessed. Union Jack eventually passed to Eastern National in December 1936 for £25,000, of which about £8,000 was subsequently attributable to London Transport's share.

Fred England retained an interest in a haulage business, but, following his final withdrawal from the bus business, immediately became involved in a new idea: hire purchase for motorcars! Quite the businessman!

4

THE NUTTALL YEARS
1931–1939

The tram track was due for a complete renewal in 1930. Consideration was given to rebuilding and extending the system with double tracks where possible, as well as updating the cars, but no decision was made. Discussions were held with ENOC that they provide replacement buses in return for an agreed annual payment. In early 1931 an offer of £64,000 was finally made by ENOC for the 'goodwill only', leaving the corporation to dispose of the tramcars, remove the track and re-instate the roads. Part of the arrangement was that Ronald Nuttall, then the tramway engineer and manager, would be given a suitable position with a salary of £500 P/A. The company also agreed to take over as many of the employees as was possible. The corporation, however, would have to covenant not to engage in any form of passenger transport for a period of twenty-one years.

The council approved the deal with ENOC on 20 January 1931, accepted by seventeen votes to seven. On the strength of this, Eastern National ordered ten Leyland Titans. However, local residents (Luton Ratepayers Association) were not so happy. A petition followed, and the deal was referred back to the council, who despite public displeasure again approved the matter. The Ministry of Transport was consulted, and they declared that the deal did not come within the terms of the 1870 Tramways Act, section 44, by reason that the sale of 'goodwill only' was not permitted.

All of this caused considerable controversy within the community and the council. Even the two local newspapers (owned by the same firm) took opposing sides in the argument. *Luton News* was in favour, *Saturday Telegraph* was opposed. ENOC were requested to submit a further offer, including one for the entire undertaking as it stood. This they refused to do as they had already committed themselves to some £24,000 of expenditure on the new vehicles, together with a garage extension in anticipation of the earlier deal that had been agreed.

In June 1931 ENOC took delivery of ten of the sixteen Strachen-bodied Leyland Titan TD1's, due for delivery that year. It is believed that six of these were delivered to Luton and four to the Bedford depot, the remaining six going to the Chelmsford area. Those delivered to Luton were received with destination blinds displaying the points covered by Luton Tramways! Early in 1932 four AEC Renowns, also ordered by ENOC, again in anticipation, were delivered to Luton with similar destination blinds. The Renowns were initially used by Eastern National on their heavily trafficked routes in Luton, but were later transferred to the Chelmsford ENOC depot.

The Ministry of Transport meanwhile advised the corporation not to dispose of its undertaking. As a consequence the corporation then applied for licences to operate buses. The corporation was confident that their proposed routes, largely based upon the old tram routes, would be agreed upon, and invited tenders for five single-deck and four double-deck low-bridge buses. These were to run on three routes, one to partly replace the Dunstable Road tram route, extending to Chaul End Lane, another to run from Cutenhoe Road to Biscot Mill, and the third to run from central Luton to Round Green, again similar to the old tram route. The application to the East Midland Traffic Commissioner was declined, having been opposed by ENOC, XL Motor Services of Dunstable, Bluebird Services and National. Tenders were received for complete vehicles from AEC, Daimler, Dennis and Leyland. The offer from Daimler with Duple bodies was not only the most competitive

11. One of the Leyland Titans outside the works (TM3724) that ENOC ordered in anticipation!

12. AEC Renown ordered by ENOC for work in Luton, later transferred to Chelmsford depot.

but also included a re-training programme for tram drivers, and was accepted. Daimler attempted to persuade the corporation to use their newly developed 'Poppet Valve' engine (mentioned later). The commissioners made it clear that they would consider a scheme to substitute buses for trams. This was submitted, but again opposed by ENOC and XL, who both maintained that an additional bus operator was not necessary, and that they could easily provide any extra transport required if trams ceased to operate. The commissioners did not uphold their objections, and the corporation was able to commence running nine buses to replace two tram routes on 1 March 1932 on the Dunstable Road and London Road/Wardown services. Initially buses Nos 1–5 replaced trams on the London Road–Wardown route, whilst Nos 6–9 replaced trams on the Dunstable Road route. Replacement of the Round Green service was delayed until extra double-deck buses were delivered.

LCT was fortunate in obtaining a licence to substitute buses for trams. This permission was given under the relaxed procedures of the Road Traffic Act of 1930. This avoided a specific Bill of Parliament, which would have otherwise cost the corporation a good deal of time and money.

Route Details:

(Note: no route numbers at this time)

Commenced: 01/03/32

Dunstable Road route: Running from Bailey Street to Beechwood Road/Waller Avenue, this was similar to the former tram route, but extended by about half a mile toward Waller Avenue. By May frequency was every twenty minutes, and every forty minutes on Sundays, with additional weekday journeys to Vauxhall Motors and Electrolux. These services became routes 1, 2, 3 and 4.

Wardown route: Similar to former tram route, extended by a few hundred yards at both ends, the Cutenhoe Road–Stockingstone Road service ran at a frequency of every fifteen minutes. This became route 7.

Commenced: 17/04/32

Round Green route: Differed slightly from the original tram route in so far as terminus was now on Williamson Street, going outwards via Mill Street, and inwards via Williamson Street.

This Luton (Library)–Round Green service ran at a frequency, by May 1933, of every twenty minutes, with an hourly extension to Stopsley Green. When numbering was introduced services became 10 to Round Green and 11 to Stopsley.

A further three Daimler double-deckers finally replaced all the trams on 17 April 1932. Buses 10–12 then commenced services on the Round Green route. As we have already noted, the last tram ran on 16 April 1932, the previous night. Ronald H. Nuttall, known as 'Harry', the tramway engineer and manager, became the general manager of LCT.

The tramways, although in decline in latter years, had generally been operated at a profit, thus enabling the bus undertaking to commence without outstanding debts. To acquire additional vehicles, loan monies were made available by the Ministry.

By June 1932 a further two double-deck buses entered service, enabling LCT to successfully tender for contract journeys to Vauxhall, the Chaul End Lane factories and Electrolux. Many factories at that time did not have canteen facilities, meaning that local workers needed to return home for lunch. The corporation successfully applied to convert the Beechwood Road–Vauxhall and Bailey Street–Electrolux routes to peak hour stage carriages with restrictions. Another single-deck was ordered and, at the same time, an application was made to the Traffic Commissioners for a new weekday circular service from Park Square, through High Town, Hart Lane and Crawley Green Road to Park Square. This raised objections from ENOC, which resulted in an amended application which became the Russell Rise–Hart Lane circular service. Other services applied for covered the Farley Hill–Stockingstone Road route, introduced in April 1933.

Negotiations, meanwhile, continued with Fred England. Application was made by the corporation for licences to initially operate the Bluebird routes. In anticipation of a deal, England would not

13. Daimlers: a pre-delivery photograph at Duple Coachworks.

14. Daimler CH6 Duple B32R, no.3. Pre-operational photograph. Delivered 1932.

15. Combined picture of tram No.13 and one of the new Duple Daimlers.

split the business. The corporation then sought licences for all routes controlled by England's enter-prise at that time under the names of Union Jack (Luton) Omnibus Co. Ltd, XL Motor Services and Bluebird Services.

Agreement was reached at £21,000 during late October 1932. The deal was for England's total bus interests, and included fourteen single-deck buses, one chassis and one double-deck bus, all with manual gearboxes, leased premises at Wardown Garage, Luton, and use of England's family premises between Britain Street and Lovers Walk, Dunstable, and the offices at 2 Bridge Street, and 5 Manchester Street in Luton. All staff up to and including traffic manager Ernest Savage and mem-bers of the Hinds family were to be transferred into LCT employment. The fleet were owned either in the name of Fred England (t/a 'XL Service') or by Union Jack (Luton) Ltd (t/a 'Union Jack' or Bluebird). England retained the Ltd Co. title which, as we mentioned earlier, he was to use for the acquisition of a new bus business in Bedford.

ENOC had, meanwhile, sought talks on future agreements with the corporation. A twenty-one-year agreement was eventually signed between ENOC and LCT at midnight on 30 November 1932, effective from 1 December 1932, known as the 'Midnight Agreement' – but not before further contention concerning the acquisition of England's operation. This agreement nevertheless settled the basis of future operations in the area by both operators.

Naturally, when details of LCT's earlier application for licences to operate England's routes emerged, ENOC objected to the application which they believed contravened their earlier agreement. A new player now entered the scene, LPTB, as there were routes outside the borough; LPTB were forbidden to carry local passengers in Luton and Dunstable. A public enquiry took place and several of the more contentious applications were withdrawn. No doubt this arose as a result of some back room dealing, as agreement in principle had been reached by the time the hearing commenced, although the hearing itself was lengthy.

ENOC had serious objections because the corporation would, if granted permission, have been able to operate to Houghton Regis, Dunstable, Leighton Buzzard, Whipsnade Zoo, Pegsdon and Tring, all of these places being well outside the borough boundary. However, LCT were not restricted solely to the borough boundary, and within the terms of the 'Midnight Agreement', were

16. Daimler CH6 Duple L26/26R, no.6. Pre-operation photo. The first double-deck bus owned by the corporation. Delivered 1932.

17. Daimler CH6 Willowbrook, No.19, L26/26R. Delivered 1933.

18. This low-bridge Daimler, strangely a victim of a very low bridge perhaps! This photograph clearly shows the double gangway on the upper-deck. The blind indicator identifies this bus as one of those delivered between 1934 and 1936.

19. Daimler COG5's lined up in the depot. No.22 in the foreground.

able to operate to Dunstable, Houghton Regis, Streatley, Bramingham Turn (Old Bedford Road)
and Stopsley (Hitchin Road). These arrangements meant that both operators duplicated services
on part of some routes. The Traffic Commissioners granted protection to the corporation on those
routes covered by the old trams where they were permitted intermediate stage fares, whilst ENOC
were not. Other duplicated routes remained competitive. In January 1933 a further two double-
decker buses were ordered to permit the extension of the Round Green service to Stopsley, under
the terms of the 'Midnight Agreement'. These were ordered, as well as two new single-deck buses, in
anticipation of the acquisition of England's businesses.

The full list of services LCT was able to obtain licences for are listed later in this chapter, the
remainder being allocated as shown to ENOC in exchange for some small transfers to LCT. These
changes took effect, along with the purchase of Fred England's interest, on 23 March 1933, but only
after a lengthy traffic court hearing, during which time the upgrading of the Bluebird fleet continued, replacing the small fourteen to twenty-seat vehicles with thirty-one to thirty-two-seat vehicles
which were acquired second-hand or leased.

Route Situation from 23 March 1933   Became

Former XL Motor Services passed to Luton Corporation

Luton (Library)–Houghton Regis–Dunstable (Great North Road)		LC 6

Former Bluebird Services passed to Luton Corporation

Luton (Manchester Square)	–Leagrave (week-days)	LC 13
„ „	–Biscot Mill (week-days)	LC 14
„ „	–Stockingstone Road (week-days)	LC 15
„ „	–Colin Road (week-days)	LC 12
„ „	–Hexton and Pegsdon	
	to Bramingham Turn	LC 16
	–Remainder of route ENOC 12A	
„ „	Whipsnade Zoo (Sundays and	
	Bank Holidays) (to Dunstable)	LC 19
„ „	–Remainder of route ENOC 53B	

Former Union Jack (Luton) Omnibus Co. Ltd passed to Luton Corporation

Luton (Albert Road)	–Vauxhall Works contract	
	(application for licence 11/33)	LC 18
Luton (Library)	–Whipsnade Zoo (to Dunstable only)	LC 5

Former XL Motor Services passed to ENOC

Luton (Library)	–Dunstable–Leighton Buzzard–Wing	ENOC 18
Leighton Buzzard	–Tring	ENOC 18

Former Bluebird Services passed to ENOC

Luton (Manchester Square)	–Bramingham Turn	LC 16
	–Remainder of route	ENOC 12A
" "	–Whipsnade Zoo (Sundays only)	
	to Dunstable	LC 19
„ „	–Remainder of route	ENOC 53B

Former Union Jack (Luton) Omnibus Co. Ltd passed to ENOC

Luton (Vauxhall)	–Leighton Buzzard	ENOC
		ext. 18

Enlarged LCT Routes after Acquisition with Route Numbers Allocated During 1933

	Route	Frequency	Origin
1.	Luton (Bailey Street)–Beechwood Road (ext. Waller Ave. 06/33)	Daily	Tram 01/03/32
2.	Beechwood Road–Vauxhall (ext. to Waller Ave.6/33)	M–F	Cont. until/ Stage 05/32
3.	Luton (Bailey Street)–Electrolux	M–F	Cont. until/ Stage 5/32
4.	Luton (Park Square)–Chaul End Lane	M–F	Stage 01/34
5.	Luton (Bailey Street) (Park Square)–Beechwood Road	Daily	Tram route
6.	Luton (Library)–Dunstable (Town Hall)	Daily	ex–UJ
7.	Luton (Library)–Houghton Regis–Dunstable	Daily	ex–XL
8.	Luton (Bailey Street)–Stockingstone Road	Daily	Tram 01/03/32
9.	Farley Hill–Stockingstone Road	M–F	Intro. 04/33
10.	Russell Rise–Hart Lane (Circular)	Daily	Intro. 12/10/32
11.	Luton (Library)–Round Green (Peak as 11)	M–F	Tram 17/04/32
12.	Luton (Library)–Round Green–Stopsley	Daily	Intro. 01/04/33
13.	Luton (Manchester Square)–Colin Road	Daily	ex–BB
14.	Luton (Manchester Square)–Biscot Mill–Leagrave	M–F	ex–BB
15.	Luton (Manchester Square)–Biscot Mill	Daily	ex–BB
16.	Luton (Manchester Square)–Old Bedford Road– Biscot Mill	Sun	ex–BB
17.	Luton (Manchester Square)–Bramingham Turn	M–F	ex–BB
18.	Richmond Hill–Vauxhall Works	M–F	(Ex-Contract) Intro '33
19.	Albert Road–Vauxhall Works	M–F	(Ex-Contract) Intro '33
20.	Luton (Manchester Square)–Leagrave–Dunstable	Sun	ex. BB

The livery of the buses was maroon, with white window surrounds with bands beneath them, a silver roof and black mudguards and wheels. 'Luton Corporation' fleet name was located in the centre of the lower white window surround each side of the vehicle, with the corporation coat of arms located centrally on the lower saloon panels. The five Willowbrook-bodied Daimlers had a longer fleet name, and the double-decks 18 and 19 had a more steeply raked front end.

Reference to the Appendix fleet list will show those buses which were acquired before the England acquisition and those acquired by Fred England's business. It has to be said that the routes were clearly more important than the buses, most of which did not stay in service for very long. A total of sixteen vehicles were taken over, but only eleven were retained and given fleet Nos 20–29 and 40.

Vehicles acquired were:

1 × 50 double-deck Dennis Lance LCT 28
9 × 32 single-deck Dennis LCT 20–26, 29 and 40
1 × 31 single-deck Dennis LCT 27
4 × 20 single-deck Dennis G Disposed
1 × 14 single-deck Chevrolet Disposed

Ownership of some of the vehicles was initially disputed. It seems that one, or possibly two, of the thirty-two-seat single-deck Dennis, Nos 21, 22 or 29, left the fleet in March 1934. One of these may have been the disputed vehicle/s on lease to England from Manchester Corporation. As a point of interest, before passing to England, LCT Nos 20 and 29 were originally Manchester

20. LCT acquired vehicles Nos 25, 27, and 24, pictured after withdrawal at Park Street depot in 1937.

21. LCT, formerly owned by England, acquired by LCT. No.21, Dennis EV Strachen B32D, in new LCT livery.

Corporation Nos 141 and 142. LCT 22 had belonged to W.D. Beaumont of Enfield. LCT 24 and one unlicensed Dennis, G reg. RO 9518, were originally owned by Chiltern Bus Co. (E. Prentice & Son) of Tring, RO 9518 came to Union Jack via Red Rose of Wendover, and LCT 24 direct to Union Jack. LCT 27 originally belonged to Twines of Eastbourne, then Southdown Motor Services before passing to Union Jack. Around March 1933, two of the twenty-seated vehicles were acquired by England for his Union Jack (Luton) Omnibus Co. operating in Bedford, following his purchase of Carding's business. The other two went to a dealer. PSV records do not show the fate of the Chevrolet. In November 1933 an application was made to convert Vauxhall contract services 17 and 18 to stage carriage services. At the same time an extension of service 7 to Ludlow Avenue was refused.

Following experiments during the previous months, route numbers were approved in December 1933 for introduction as soon as possible. Many of the routes inherited from Bluebird in March 1933 terminated in Manchester Square. The number of corporation buses which would collect at this point on different services probably lead to the introduction of service numbers, although this practice was already common amongst other operators. The story goes that people were simply confused and were often getting on the wrong buses. In May 1933 plate holders were introduced to the front nearside windows, upstairs for double-deck buses.

Following an arbitration award on 18 January 1934, LCT was granted an extension to Chaul End Lane on service 4, as well as services to New Bedford Road Greyhound Track and an extension of service 7 when suitable. In July 1934 the ticket office at 5 Manchester Street was vacated and temporarily moved to the Horse & Jockey snack bar, modified as a ticket office. A modified inspector's hut in Williamson Street became the replacement ticket office. Again, in July 1934, fixed stopping places were finally introduced on former Bluebird Services, already in operation on other services. In order to alleviate congestion one-way traffic was introduced in Williamson Street and Bridge Street.

Harry Nuttall, the general manager, is recorded as having refused a request for the buses to carry adverts. Throughout his time he continually refused further requests, probably because the trams had been festooned with advertisements, a practice he clearly found distasteful. However, all ex-England vehicles carried advertisements as their contracts had not been terminated upon acquisition. The Park Street depot expanded on to the sewage destructor site adjacent, and the depot entrance was widened. A sub-committee was formed to investigate exchange of services between LCT and ENOC.

Construction of a new paint shop had been completed by 26 June 1934. In September 1934 several drivers were warned of 'driving at excessive speeds'. Two Daimler CP6 single-deckers entered service on 11 September 1934.

With the exception of the ex-England vehicles, the pre-war fleet was standardised on Daimler chassis with, initially, Duple bodies which were later changed to Willowbrook. New vehicles were ordered from the chassis manufacturer who sub-contracted the bodywork. These low-bridge double-deck buses were of an established design with twin sunken gangways around limited upper-deck seating. This had been considered more suitable in view of the ease of access they afforded and the shorter journey times for most passengers. Seats were arranged in eight rows of three, with two directly in front of the upper rear window and an additional sunken gangway in front of these rear seats and across the front seats. This meant that the roof height of the driver's cab was very low, as was the platform ceiling. There are stories that drivers would place cushions in the roof of their cab to stop them banging their heads! Luton was probably the last operator to specify this type of design as the single drop right-hand gangway was by now in general use. All Daimler double-decks numbered up to seventy, apart from one (mentioned later), had this design. By March 1934 the fleet comprised thirty-five vehicles, eleven of which had been acquired from Fred England, the remaining twenty-four being new from manufacturers.

An article published by *The Commercial Motor* in 1934 gives some interesting statistics showing that in the last year of tram operation, 1931/32, the working expenses per car mile, including power costs, amounted to 10.8p, with receipts at 15.48p. In the first year of bus operation, 1932/33, expenses were 11.24p and receipts 16.42p per mile. In neither case was capital cost included. The article also mentioned that in the final year of tram operation 2,932,912 passengers were carried, in contrast to the first year of bus operation when there were 4,685,899. The additional services did not appear in the accounts until the following year, thereby demonstrating how usage had increased with the introduction of buses. The greater speed was at the time attributed to this increase in usage. However, average tram speed was 6mph, buses only 2mph faster. The following year accounts showed an increase in usage by 1.5 million.

22. Inside the Park Street depot. Cleaning the buses.

23. Rather a wide-angle lens, but a good 'line up' in the thirties..

24. Rear view of a Daimler in Manchester Street.

25. Single-deck Daimler in Bedford Road.

26. An apprentice working on a Daimler pre-selector.

When the original order was placed by the corporation for buses in 1931 the lowest tender received was from Daimler. Despite this, it is interesting to consider other reasons given in an article published by the *Commercial Motor* in 1934 as to why Daimler was finally chosen. However, although we cannot ignore the fact that Daimler were the lowest tender, it is not unreasonable to assume that Daimler tendered at near cost, aware that, like many other municipalities, tram drivers found it easier to make the transfer to self-changing gearboxes, they knew that once committed it could be the forerunner to future orders, as, of course, it proved to be in Luton's case.

The Daimler had a fluid flywheel, and self-changing gearbox. It was selected on account of its ease of control. The corporation wished to keep its tramway employees, all but one of whom succeeded in obtaining a licence to drive a public service vehicle with this type of transmission.

27. Daimlers at the depot.

An extract from the article reads as follows:

Looking back on the decision made more than two years ago, Mr R.H. Nuttall, the transport manager, has no cause to regret his committee's choice; in fact he tells us that maintenance expenses on the fluid flywheels and self changing gearboxes have been considerably less than would have been the case with ordinary clutches and lay shaft type gearboxes.

This is attributed mainly to the absence of transmission shocks, and is of importance when one considers that some quite steep gradients are encountered on the routes, also that seven or eight stops per mile are made in this particularly busy town, which is hedged by hills.

At this time Daimler buses were a familiar sight in many provincial towns and cities. Daimler was a popular choice. Their success was linked with the company's successful combination of two inventions: the pre-selective epicycle gearbox, the brainchild of Walter Gordon Wilson, and the fluid coupling produced under Vulcan-Sinclair patents. The pre-selective gearbox had been the subject of experiments on a Vauxhall car by Tilling Stevens in the twenties before being taken up by Armstrong Siddeley. The fluid flywheel gave a perfectly smooth start under all conditions, but could not free the drive completely, as was necessary for a satisfactory change with an orthodox gearbox. By marrying the two, Daimler solved all problems and produced a most effective transmission system.

First or second gear could be engaged with the vehicle at rest or idling. The next gear required could be selected at any time while in advance, the actual change occurring when the gear-engaging pedal was activated. Gear changes were foolproof, and could be made without any skill, so that engine braking was always available, although a moderate degree of timing was needed for smooth changes. The system, although complex, proved very reliable, with many municipalities undertaking tramway replacement, requiring vehicles that could be driven by former tram drivers. Three Daimler CH type with pre-selective systems had been supplied to LGOC in July 1930 and had been very successful; so much so, in fact, that the system became the standard for London buses for two decades. Daimler made all pre-selective gearboxes for use in AEC chassis up until 1934.

Daimler experimented with Gardner engines in 1932 and by 1933 the first Gardner-engined Daimlers were in service, designated COG5. The Luton delivery in 1932 was, apart from one Daimler CP6 (No.7), fitted with Daimler 5.76-litre sleeve valve petrol engines, CH6. No.7, and later 21, 22, 38 and 39 had Daimler CP6 engines. These were indiscernible from the CH6 externally, but had a

28. No.34 delivered in 1933, pictured at Vauxhall, probably about 1950. It looks likely it is working service 4 extended from Park Square.

poppet-valve petrol engine, hence the 'P'. The first COG5, LCT No.20 (single-deck), was delivered in February 1935. This particular bus was leased until 21 March 1935, when the council approved the purchase of the trial vehicle.

These buses had a five-cylinder 7.0-litre 5LW power unit, 85bhp at 1,700rpm, and a Daimler chassis with Gardner diesel engines. Buses delivered before 1936 had rigid engine mountings, which caused considerable vibration – post 1936, buses had a very effective flexible engine mounting which, thankfully, solved this problem.

In passing I will mention the COG6, although LCT did not take delivery of any of these double-deckers. Again, these had Gardner engines of 6LW, 8.4 litres, developing 102bhp at 1,700rpm. With their flexible engine mounting the vehicle was amongst the most refined pre-war double-deckers in terms of smoothness.

The single-deck version of the COG5 was, until 1936, very similar to the double-decker in layout and appearance, having a 17ft 6in wheelbase.

At this time there was growing interest in maximum passenger carrying capacity, and to meet this within the 27ft 6in length limit a new version, designated COG5 40 instead of COG5 single-deck, as hitherto, was introduced. This had a more compact bonnet design, reverting to a vertical radiator instead of the classic sloping-fronted type so characteristic of most Daimlers. The distance from the front of the radiator to the back of the bonnet was reduced by nearly 8in, giving the model what must remain one of the most compact installations of a Gardner 5LW engine ever. In theory it was possible to accommodate forty passengers, although this seems never to have been done, most users settling for thirty-nine-seat versions. LCT's first COG5 40, No.45, was delivered in November 1935. All single-deck Daimlers subsequently delivered were of this type.

In February 1935 the council approved an additional running shed and recreation room, to be built on acquired land at the Park Street depot by local builders H.C. Janes Ltd. Work commenced in December 1935. The new running shed was to hold thirty buses. The annual report for the trading year ending February 1935 showed seventeen double-deck and twenty-three single-deck buses

29. Eastern National meets LCT. Ouch!

in stock. A new Daimler COG5 single-deck was on hire from Daimler: the first oil engine bus in the fleet, replacing an ex-England Dennis. This vehicle was purchased on 21 March 1935.

The tenancy of Wardown garage, acquired in the earlier purchase, had not been renewed on expiry on 25 March 1935, the property having been re-let by the end of September 1935. A new tenant had been found by the owners.

By March 1935, twelve months after the new paint shop had been completed, nineteen buses had been re-painted. There were 176 employees, including 128 drivers and conductors. The undertaking had shown a loss of £40 for the year 1933/34, but returned a profit of £8,500 for 1934/35. Staff were introduced to a forty-eight-hour, six-day week, with a ten-minute signing on allowance. Drivers pay stood at £2.18 p/w, conductors at £2.8 with conductors being paid more for double-deck operations.

Two further Daimler COG5 double-deckers entered service in April 1935, followed by two more in May. The Dennis Lance (28) was reconditioned by Willowbrook in June 1935 at a cost of £175, and committed to contract work thereafter. As a result of the closure of the Greyhound Stadium in New Bedford Road on 4 October 1935 there was a noticeable decline in traffic on route 16. Service 7 was extended to Culverhouse Road/St Augustine's Avenue, and the London Road terminus was moved to Cutenhoe Road.

An additional Daimler COG5 single-deck entered service in November. This was the first forty-seat single-deck, and was used to support an increased frequency for service 7.

In December 1935 additional lunchtime journeys were introduced to and from Electrolux Works as a temporary measure whilst the canteen was under construction. Service 12 was extended from Colin Road to Round Green.

In January 1936 a new service 20 was proposed between Vauxhall Works and Biscot Mill, and a further Daimler COG5 40 single-deck was delivered. It had taken until February 1936 to erect bus stop signs at recognised stopping places within the borough, but LCT refused to take responsibility for erecting those outside the borough boundary. During February Eastern National announced an increase in the frequency of services on their Leagrave and Biscot Road services. LCT countered this with an increased Saturday service on route 14, Sunday service on 13 and a revised service 19. In March two more Daimler COG5 40 single-deckers entered service, thought to be 46 and 47, and a Biscot Mill–Vauxhall Works peak hour service 20 was introduced. Service number indicators were now to be fitted to both the front and rear of the vehicles. The annual report for 1935/36 showed a

30. Cash desk at the depot.

loss of £81, the fleet had increased by eight vehicles net; staff had increased by nineteen to 195. Buses 1–40 had all been repainted during the year.

In May 1936 LCT contacted Daimler to arrange for one of the current batch of buses on order to be of single upper gangway layout with four seats per row instead of three. When Daimler asked for an extra £120 to make the necessary alteration to a partially built body, LCT withdrew the request. Willowbrook, who were responsible for the bodies at that time, produced a design for a shoulder rest for seats adjacent to the gangway. This was useful as people invariably fell off the end of the seats into the gangway on sharp corners! LCT agreed to one vehicle being fitted as an experiment. This type of seating was adopted on all future double-deck buses from Willowbrook.

It is rumoured that LCT was the last operator in the country to take double gangway double-deck buses. However, it seems that one in the batch on order in 1936 may have had a single drop gangway, believed to be No. 51, 52 or 53. It certainly wasn't No. 50 as the body of this bus was still seen derelict in Caddington, near Luton, in August 1969, although it had been broken up by January 1970.

In June 1936 four more buses were delivered, two COG5 single-deck and two COG5 double-deckers. In September services 1 and 3 were extended, but only to Seymour Avenue. Approval was gained to divert services 7 and 8 upon introduction of a one-way system in Castle Street and Chapel Street.

During the latter part of 1936 LCT began to fit uncollected fares boxes on all double-deck buses at the platform entrance. Advertising was permitted inside vehicles for bus publicity only. Two 'Auto waybill' ticket machines were introduced experimentally on Vauxhall services. Workmen's fares were still only available on former tram service routes. In October Dunstable Council requested an extension of service 6 to McManus Estate, which was refused. Concern was expressed about Saturday night 'rowdies' on buses. A new system was introduced for return tickets to be collected for an exchange ticket instead of the original being cancelled.

In November 1936 there were major service change recommendations to extend service 1 from Waller Avenue to Pembroke Avenue. Service 4 was to be augmented with part service and extended from Chaul End Lane to Lewsey Road. Service 7 was to be extended to Fountains Road directly after the road was surfaced. Service 14 was to be extended from Biscot Mill to Culverhouse Road. Service 18 was to be extended from Albert Road to Farley Hill. A new twenty-minute service was proposed between Park Square and Chaul End Lane.

There were proposals in December 1936 to operate late night buses from LMR Station in conjunction with railway excursions. These were introduced, but restricted to single-deck operations, with tickets issued in advance by the railway. Also there were proposals to operate a new works service between Vauxhall and Stopsley Green.

Other than those vehicles acquired from England, LCT had purchased only new Daimlers, apart from a new Commer 8cwt van added to the fleet in January 1937. Other additions that month were three new COG5 single-deck Daimlers enabling the Vauxhall–Stopsley peak hour service 21 to commence. Also, a new service was proposed between Biscot Mill and Kingsway.

31. The cash desk.

Percival Aircraft Ltd opened their new factory on 18 January 1937 at Luton Airport. Mr Percival approached the corporation to provide a bus service to the airport for the benefit of his employees. LCT looked into the request and concluded that the road from Kimpton Road was only suitable for a twenty-six-seat bus. LCT applied to the Traffic Commissioners for a service from Park Square to Eaton Green Road (still a country lane) terminating at the airport boundary. Following approval in February LCT extended a Vauxhall Works service to accommodate Percival Aircraft. In March 1937 LCT purchased a twenty-six-seat, petrol-driven Bedford WTB with a Duple body specifically for the airport service 23. It carried fleet No.60, reg. BBM 245. Wartime development of the airport factories and roads meant larger vehicles were used, and, as a consequence, 60 was often later seen being used by engineers. It remained with LCT until 1948, when it was sold out of service, and last seen in Rainham in 1951.

Two additional Daimler COG5 double-deckers were added to the fleet at the end of March. The proposed new service 22 was introduced on 6 April 1937 between Park Square and Chaul End Lane. It was agreed jointly with Eastern National that a new style cast-iron bus stop would be introduced within the borough of Luton for both companies. It was proposed that the Stopsley terminus for service 11 be moved to Stapleford Road as soon as roads were made up. No actual change was to occur until the post-war era. The new airport service 23 was introduced on 6 April between Park Square and Airport Approach.

On 21 April 1937 LCT had a strike on its hands, mainly over pay, but also other grievances. The strike ended five days later, on 26 April, when wages were increased by 2/6d per week. New signing on/off arrangements were agreed with a new office in Gordon Street to facilitate this arrangement. Travelling time to and from the depot was now to be paid where appropriate. A works committee was formed to discuss other grievances. Staff pay was finally brought into line with national rates in November 1937 when LCT agreed to pay road staff in accordance with National Joint Industrial Council (NJIC) union rates.

During April 1937 the Traffic Commissioner requested a revised turning arrangement in connection with the proposed extension of service 4, to run to either Skimpot or Lewsey Road. The commissioner also required that service 18 be turned at Whitehill Avenue rather than Stockwood Park Gates.

In June 1937 service 4 was introduced to Lewsey Road. The idea of a Dallow Road–Round Green service was dropped due to the narrow road over Waller Avenue Bridge. In July one of the former England Dennis single-deck buses was withdrawn. At the same time four more Daimler COG5 double-deckers were added to the fleet. In September 1937 a proposal was made to increase the frequency of service 11 with an extension along Ashcroft Road. Also, a new works service between Vauxhall and Cutenhoe Road was proposed. Furthermore, former England single-deck buses were withdrawn at the end of the month.

32. Daimler COG5 Gardner 5LW Willowbrook L26/26R No.53, delivered 1936. It is pictured later in its life after the front destination box had been altered to a single rectangular style.

In October 1937 the proposed extension of service 11 to Ashcroft Road was changed to Chesford Road, ideally to be effective as soon as the road was surfaced, when, in reality, no change was achieved until post-war, in 1947!

Percival Aircraft now requested that the new airport service 23 should include a link with the LMR Railway Station. LMR were agreeable to the use of Station Road to park buses at a notional fee of £1 per annum. As a result of this new arrangement certain buses on route 23 were now extended to Luton LMR Station.

Following the report of a sub-committee, who had examined loadings of ENOC buses serving late trains, a proposal was made in October 1937 that, on Saturdays only, buses were to meet late trains from St Pancras at 11.43 p.m. and 12.30 a.m. Three buses were each to take the following routes around the town from the station:

   i) New Bedford Road, Montrose Avenue, Culverhouse Road, Fountains Road, Stockingstone Road and Old Bedford Road.
   ii) Old Bedford Road, Cromwell Road, Biscot Road, Denbeigh Road, Leagrave Road, Grange Avenue, Leagrave High Street and Oakley Road.
   iii) New Bedford Road, Crawley Road, Bury Park Road, Dunstable Road and Lewsey Road.

Proposals to operate regular services from Station Road were refused by the borough council. A further double-deck Daimler COG5 was delivered. A proposal to run a Sunday service 9 on the Hart Lane route was rejected. Another ex-England Dennis single-deck was withdrawn and offered for sale. A further Daimler COG5 double-deck was delivered.

In January 1938 three further single-deck COG5 40 single-deck buses joined the fleet. These were to be the last single-deck buses delivered until 1967. The new works service 24 was introduced between Vauxhall and Cutenhoe Road. In February 1938 proposals to divert works services and introduce a new circular service to serve Somerset Avenue was considered, although it was deemed unsuitable due to the steep turn out of Crawley Road. It was agreed that a second-hand Daimler engine would be purchased as a spare. An evening service of a single journey was to be introduced from Dunstable Waterlow Works to Luton. In March 1938 Bertram Mills' Circus came to Luton and pitched just off Park Street. 'To & From Circus' stickers were displayed on services 1 and 3. During April 1938 the unsold ex-England single-deck was sold to Morrell of Leeds for £51. Requests to extend service 6 within Dunstable were repeatedly refused.

In June 1938 LCT commenced replacing all bus stop signs with the new style cast design showing service numbers with a common pattern for both LCT and ENOC. A further proposal was made to introduce a Sunday service on route 9. The annual report for 1936/37 showed that the fleet had increased by ten net. Now there were twenty-five single-deck and thirty-three double-deck buses. There were 234 staff, a further increase of thirty-nine over the year, which included 171 drivers and conductors. Two more experimental auto ticket machines were introduced.

Luton Airport officially opened on 16 July 1938. Use of the small Bedford had already been agreed on for service 23, but only to the borough boundary. Permission was granted for the service to be extended into the airport following agreement by the Traffic Commissioners on 7 October 1938. However, on the day of the official opening, a special bus service via Provincial Estates Road (Eaton Valley Road), with double-deck vehicles jointly operated with London Transport, were run, and minimum fare regulations on LPTB routes 364 and 383 were suspended for the day. The final delivery of four Daimler COG5 double-deck buses permitted the last three ex-England single-deck Dennis to now be held in reserve.

By February 1939 there were reports circulating of an informal meeting with ENOC on the question of a possible coordination scheme. It was agreed that the terminus for service 12 at Round Green be moved to Stockingstone Road. In April 1939 LCT agreed to permit advertising inside saloons for army recruitment only. There was pressure from local residents in Stopsley to implement the extension of a service to Ashcroft Road. Three second-hand engines were purchased from Daimler. Due to low patronage LCT sought to withdraw Saturday late night buses from the LMR Station. The Traffic Commissioners refused this in June 1939. In May 1939 it was reported that three withdrawn Dennis vehicles, 23, 26 and 40, were allocated to the corporation ARP committee (to become civil defence) to be used as mobile first-aid units.

In December 1939 a proposal was made to run an additional service on route 23 during summer evenings from May to September and weekend afternoons. A request from the Traffic Commissioner to extend service 6 in Dunstable was refused by LCT.

The Daimler petrol sleeve valve engine buses were becoming unreliable. Spares were proving difficult. When breakdowns occurred they were usually out of service for a while. By this time the fleet had expanded to seventy, and operated over twenty-four routes, details of which are given at the end of this publication.

In May 1939 it was clear that general manager Harry Nuttall could no longer continue due to a deterioration of his health. His doctor's certificate reported that he was 'incapable of discharging duties with efficiency due to ill health.' His services were terminated on 31 July 1939. Ernest Savage (ex-Bluebird) was his deputy, and held the post temperarily. Since joining LCT he had remained suspicious of ENOC's intentions, probably one reason that he was not seen as a likely successor. LCT advertised for a new general manager at a salary of £650 P/A, rising to £800. The new appointee was Mr C.S.A. Wickens who had been with Sheffield, and previously LGOC and LPTB. He took up his post on 5 August 1939. It was well known that he did not encourage people to use his first name, and was referred to as 'Wick'. Blackout regulations were enforced in September 1939; revised schedules were then introduced reducing regular services, especially during blackout, with increases in works services.

For some reason only known to themselves, the Warden Hill Ratepayers Association wanted the Bramingham Turn destination changed on route 16. It seems that this never happened. Restrictions remained on ENOC to pick up fare-paying passengers in the central part of Luton, on George Street and Upper George Street, owing to original Luton Tramway agreements.

Fleet Summary as at 31 July 1939

Petrol engines	d/d	s/d
Daimler CH6	8	6
Daimler CP6	14	4
Dennis Lance	1	
Bedford WTB	1	
Oil engines	**d/d**	**s/d**
Daimler COG5	21	12
Total	**45**	**22**

33. Daimler COG5 Gardner 5LW Willowbrook L26/26R seen on service 6 in a livery seen between the pre-war and early post–war years.

34. Fleet Nos 61 and 64. Daimler COG5s delivered in 1937, toward the end of their useful lives.

35. Venerable line up outside Vauxhall Ministry of Transportors. Three LCT Daimlers, on works services.

36. Bedford WTB Duple, reg. BBM 245 B26F, No.60.

5

THE WAR AND BEYOND
1940–1949

War had been declared against Germany on 1 September 1939. In January 1940 a war bonus of 4s p/w. was introduced, which was to increase frequently, and was added to all staff wages. Reduced lighting was introduced to all vehicles as soon as practical. A spare Daimler chassis was purchased from Silvertown Coaches Ltd of London. In February 1940 the council agreed in principal to allow commercial advertising on vehicles for the first time, and entered discussions with agents Frank Mason and Henry Squire & Co. During earlier years, as well as prohibiting advertising, Harry Nuttall had refused to allow boards to be carried on service 7 indicating 'To and from Swimming Pool'. This was now introduced. An advertising contract was placed with Henry Squire & Co. for the duration of the war. The arrangement was that LCT would receive 75 per cent of the revenue, but be responsible for all artwork on vehicles. Unusually, adverts were painted onto the vehicles.

In March 1940 Ronald Rogers was appointed from Eastern National Chelmsford as chief schedules clerk. This released an inspector and two conductors for normal duties. A new rolling stock supervisor was sought and Mr R. Macaulay was appointed on 15 May 1940 from Southern National at Weymouth where he had been the chief engineer's assistant.

Contention over service issues still existed between LCT and ENOC despite the 'Midnight Agreement', reached on 30 November 1932. LC's application to extend the Electrolux service to Leagrave 'Sugar Loaf', to operate service 1 along Park Street to Cutenhoe Road and divert some Dunstable journeys via Selbourne Road was declined by the Traffic Commissioner. With the 'call up' of many of the regular drivers and conductors, authority was given in May 1940 for recruitment of women conductors 'if necessary'! A programme of strengthening the lightweight bodies of the double-deck Daimlers was commenced. Some of those that received this benefit were also given new square front indicator blinds. Workman's fares were made available on work's journeys operating on a Sunday.

Two severe enemy air attacks, probably intended for the airport or Vauxhall Motors, who were building Churchill tanks and QL series 4x4 army trucks, hit Park Street depot on 30 August 1940.

The first attack was on a Friday afternoon when two staff were killed and one vehicle destroyed, fleet No.19. Other damage was restricted as most of the fleet were out on the road. The second attack, by a parachute mine, on the evening of Sunday 22 September damaged a good deal of the fleet, the offices, the garage roof and nearby properties.

Fleet No.29 was destroyed and, in all, forty-six other vehicles were rendered unfit for service until their bodywork had been re-built. Two of these were lost in October 1940, Nos 2 and 22, whilst being re-built at Thurgoods of Ware, as a result of a stray bomb which landed between the two Luton buses. After these raids, the fleet was dispersed around the town throughout the night. The service was maintained as far as possible by the use of hired buses. LCT managed to borrow the ENOC reserve fleet from Clacton area in order to resume services the following Monday. The borrowed buses were all Bristols, quite a challenge for drivers who were used to the Daimler self-changing gearboxes. Maintenance work had to be carried out in the open air whilst premises were repaired.

37. Mr C.S.A. Wickens (standing)
and his traffic superintendent,
Mr R. Rogers

38. War damage, August 1940.

39. Depot war damage.
Could be No.29!

40. A Conductress on the
platform of a Daimler.

In December 1940 school buses were introduced to run to Luton Modern School and Luton High School from Cutenhoe Road and Chaul End Lane. In March 1941, in keeping with a scheme set up in Birmingham, LCT requested volunteer platform conductors to undertake platform duties whilst regular conductors collected fares. Regular passengers came forward for this role. At the same time LCT sought to recruit women drivers for single-deck buses, as well as conductors to supplement the shortfall in staffing.

During April 1941 time clocks in use on service 7 and some other services were withdrawn. In June 1941 the military authorities requisitioned buses No.3 and 17. Dunstable Town Council pressed LCT to extend Dunstable services southwards to serve the Empire Rubber Co. LCT declined this however; by October 1941 the Transport Commission had instructed LCT to provide a peak hour extension of service 6 to Empire Rubber Co. At some stage the previously extended airport service 23 to Luton LMR Station was cut back to Park Square for the duration of the war.

The wartime economy officially gave birth to the austerity bus, otherwise known as the utility bus. War had changed priorities and many materials used for construction of buses were either impossible or difficult to obtain. Together with rationing, the idea of 'making do with less' became the norm. Some manufacturers were able to continue to use materials from old stock, so most buses appeared almost as normal in 1940, but by early 1941, due to war requirements, production had almost ceased entirely. And yet, new buses were still needed, especially in areas where factory workers, essential for the war effort, needed transport, such as Luton.

In 1941 the Ministry of Supply and Ministry of War Transport, together with those in the industry, specified standards for buses to be produced during this difficult period. At this time some manufacturers still had frozen stocks of chassis. Leyland, AEC, Bristol and Dennis between them had around 430 chassis, of which some 370 were double-deck. The Leyland Titan TD7 provided almost 200 vehicles. A purchase licensing system was introduced which lasted until the end of the war. Along with other operators LCT had to apply for a license to purchase a vehicle. Ultimately the Ministry had the final say, mostly dictated by the need to support the war effort. Like other operators, LCT was obliged to accept unfamiliar chassis. Unfortunately, LCT had historically relied on Daimler, who were not amongst the major suppliers at this time. In all seventeen utility buses were purchased by LCT, allocated between 1942 and 1945. The first four buses were delivered in May 1942, all being Leyland TD7 Titans with fifty-three-seat low-bridge bodies by Brush.

These turned out to be the 'black sheep' of the fleet. They had Leyland 8.6-litre engines with a friction clutch, but a very heavy flywheel which gave them good high revs on country runs but were most unsuitable for the short hilly journeys around Luton. They were not town buses. In August 1942 Mr C. Wickens was most impressed by a proposed post-war Crossley with a teak frame and an automatic gearbox – an impression later to be regretted!

In September 1941 women drivers were introduced and paid 90 per cent of the male rate for the first six months. Perimeter seating was tried experimentally in one single-deck bus to allow thirty standing passengers. Which bus exactly is not known. R. Macaulay was promoted to deputy general manager and chief engineer, at a salary of £375 P/A.

During November 1941 staircase mirrors were first fitted to the double-deck buses. The corporation were allocated five double-deck low-bridge chassis by the Ministry of Supply. In late 1941 LCT unsuccessfully bid for fifteen high-bridge Weymann Daimlers.

In January 1942 services 5 and 6 were extended to Kensworth Lane at peak times. In April a decision was made to fit platform chairs to all double-deck buses. I presume this was to permit a passenger to sit, rather than the conductor! This was not undertaken as far as I am aware.

Attempts were made to run service 21 via Eaton Valley Road, but this proved not to be possible as the road remained privately owned. In early 1942 LCT placed an order for fifteen Daimler chassis to be matched with Metro Cammell Weymann (MCW) all-metal fifty-six-seat high-bridge bodies, to be delivered within six months of the reversion to peacetime production. This order for Daimler chassis was cancelled in September 1945. During early 1942 an AEC demonstrator was loaned from AEC Ltd, no doubt due to the pre-selector gearbox. The vehicle itself, RT19, was owned by LPTB and painted in LPTB green. It was returned in May 1942.

A fifth austerity bus, a Bristol K5G with Duple body, arrived around August 1942. This had a 7-litre Gardner oil engine. This bus, No.75, had originally been intended for Hicks Bros of Braintree, but was diverted. It only had a single destination blind at the front, so a side box was fitted in 1951.

From about mid-1943 the upper saloon rear emergency exits were permitted to be glazed, having been panelled since the end of 1940 – interestingly, about the same time wooden slatted seats were introduced, which may be remembered by those unfortunate enough to have sat on them, for they were generally quite uncomfortable. Nos 84–87 had slatted seats.

There was a restriction on panel beating, which explains the angular corners of the front and rear roof corners. Records show that the majority of double-deck utility/austerity buses in the country were high-bridge fifty-six (thirty/twenty-six) seaters. Due to its low bridges Luton had an unusually high proportion of the low-bridge variety which were being produced with fifty-five (twenty-seven/twenty-eight) seats. To preserve fuel a substantial reduction in the number of bus stops was undertaken in August 1942. By September the sales of weekly tickets on vehicles discontinued, to be in the future available through ticket agents only. In October 1942 Ronald Rogers was promoted to traffic superintendent to replace Ernest Rodgers, who was transferred to public cleansing. By November it was agreed that uncollected fare boxes were to be fitted on all double-deck buses. Enforced shortages, both of vehicles, fuel and tyres, meant many evening and Sunday services were reduced or cancelled. Priority had to be given to provide workers with transport. Many journeys at peak times were restricted to weekly or seasonal ticket holders only.

Eight further utility vehicles arrived in 1943. These were four Guy Arabs and four Daimler CWG5s (Commercial Wartime chassis with Gardner 5LW engines) with Brush bodies, for which there was no alternative. These Daimler vehicles were popular with drivers as they had the pre-selector fluid flywheel-type transmission with which drivers were familiar. Guy had been asked by the Ministry of Supply to produce 500 bus chassis, it is believed as a result of a cancelled military order for lorries. The four Guy Arabs, again with Gardner 5LW engines and Brush bodies, had Guy four-speed sliding mesh gearboxes, which proved temperamental. By 1951 these vehicles were seen on fewer duties, but were often used on route 52D, shared with ENOC. The last wartime deliveries of these utility/austerity buses were four Bristol K6A vehicles with Park Royal bodies and AEC 7.7-litre petrol engines. Two were delivered in 1944, and two in 1945. It was uncommon for such a small fleet to be allocated so many utility buses. Justification may have been a combination of the importance of Luton as a manufacturing town and the unreliability of the ageing petrol-engined Daimler fleet. With these austerity/utility buses came changes in the livery, which hitherto existed in various shades of dark red. The upper-deck on some became cream with an upper band lining in red.

41. LCT No.73, Leyland TD7 8.6 litre, L27/28R Brush.

42. Lower saloon of low-bridge utility.

43. Upper saloon of low-bridge utility.

44. Slatted seats on the upper-deck of high-bridge utility 84–87.

45. LCT No.79 Guy Arab Gardner 5LW Brush L27/28R 7 ltre.

46. LCT No.78 in the depot yard later in its life.

In February 1943 works services 17 and 21 were restricted to weekly ticket holders only. In March further reductions in bus stops were undertaken to preserve fuel. In April Mr C. Wickens was appointed local controller of fuel supplies. In June works service 2 was restricted to weekly ticket holders. Leagrave bus stops were co-ordinated with ENOC. In the September there was a review with the contractors who hand-painted the external adverts. This agreement was extended by three years until 1946.

Economies had been attempted in 1943 when experiments were made attaching gas trailers to a single-deck bus to save petrol. No. 5 was so converted for the duration of the experiment, which was discontinued when it was not found possible to achieve sufficient power to climb the hills at adequate speed.

There are reports that some single-deckers were converted to perimeter seating, although it is not known which ones. The Regional Transport Committee ordered further large-scale reductions in the number of bus stops.

The LPTB had made it known in November 1943 that it could not continue to provide a service to the villages of Studham and Kensworth. In June 1944 the Ministry of Transport requested the corporation operate a peak hour service to these villages deep within LPTB territory. This it did, extending some service 5 trips from Dunstable. The permit for this service expired in 1950. Drivers and conductors remained in short supply, and as a result many more women joined the crews. In December 1943 the corporation received requests from residents to take over the Leagrave services operated by ENOC, as they were seen to be inadequate LCT refused. New recruits traditionally had only received 50 per cent of their wage for the first twelve working days. This practice ceased, with wages to be paid in full w.e.f. January 1944. In September 1944 works service 18 was restricted to weekly ticket holders. During the year licences were surrendered on six Daimlers, two single-decks and four double-decks. All were cannibalised for spares (Nos 1, 4, 6, 7, 8 and 12).

In November 1944 the Regional Transport Committee asked LCT to provide a twice-weekly service to serve Ashridge Hospital, well outside its territory. LCT made an offer to provide services from Luton and Dunstable. After receiving an offer from London Transport to provide a Wednesday and Sunday 352A service, the Regional Transport Committee declined the LCT offer. In December 1944 the corporation requested an allocation of four high-bridge buses. Toddington Parish Council wrote to LCT in February 1945 requesting that the corporation take over the ENOC route 54. LCT responded that this idea 'could not be entertained'. During March 1945 utility bus No. 86 was severely damaged by a falling tree whilst on route 7. There had been public complaints about a lack of side

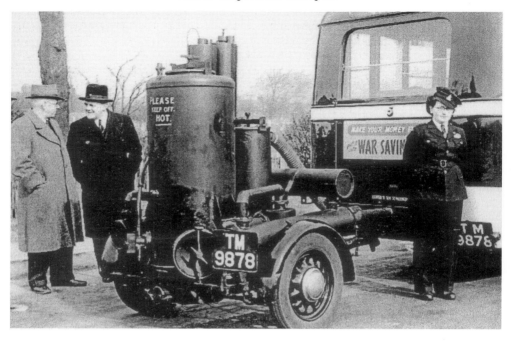

47 and 48. Daimler fleet No. 5 with gas converter.

destination blinds on austerity buses. As a result a decision was taken to remedy this in April of that year. On VE Day (9 May) services operated as normal, but staff were paid Bank Holiday rates. By May 1945 the fleet consisted of sixteen single-deck buses, plus three out of service, and fifty-two double-deckers, plus seven out of service, giving sixty-eight serviceable vehicles and a total of seventy-eight. Late in 1945 both LCT and ENOC sought service changes on routes 16 and 56-56A respectively, objecting to each other's proposals, as was usual. In August 1945 R. Macaulay departed to become general manager of Colchester Corporation.

Post-War

In September 1945, when normal ordering resumed, the earlier bid, placed in late 1941 for fifteen Daimler chassis, was cancelled. During September three double-deck Daimlers were sold for scrap (Nos 9, 10, and 11). A single-deck Daimler was converted to a utility vehicle, probably No.13. Now it seems it was the turn of Leighton Buzzard Council, who requested that LCT take over the ENOC routes 18 and 18B. Clearly passengers were not happy with ENOC operations at this time, no doubt severely hampered by vehicle shortages and a lack of trained staff – problems that all operators were experiencing. Again, LCT responded that this request 'would not be entertained'. In November LCT made an application to extend service 16 from Warden Hill to Bramingham Lane, no doubt to improve income levels. In the December LCT revised the number of standing passengers allowed. It had been eight, but this was increased to twelve during Monday-to-Friday peaks, with none in the evenings or Sundays.

Luton's immediate post-war chassis deliveries were four further Bristol K6As, which had been specifically allocated to LCT in December 1945, without bodywork The earlier deal with Weymann in 1942 for fifteen high-bridge, originally with the cancelled Daimler chassis, was still outstanding.

The order was reduced to four. This permitted them to provide the bodywork for the four Bristol K6As delivered in 1946. In fact, although I have only realised it whilst writing this chapter, they were remarkably similar to the STL Weymanns supplied to the LPTB which worked out of Watford depot and worked into Luton (Park Square) on the LPTB 321 route at that time. These were also delivered in 1945 and 1946, but, of course, were based on the AEC Regent chassis. The Luton buses did not, however, have the familiar Weymann skirt but straight lower side panels. Nos 88–91 finally arrived with their Weymann bodies in July 1946 (picture No.57 shows fleet No.89, one of these vehicles).

Early in 1945 the Ministry of Wartime Transport had informed operators that they might consider applications for Crossley chassis. This was followed later in 1945 by notice that both Leyland and AEC could be ordered, but were not necessarily available! LCT had many problems, with a demand for new and improved services new vehicles remained in short supply. Gone was the ideal established in 1933 of standardising Daimler chassis: the issue of utility vehicles during the war had put paid to that. Immediate post-war was little different; it was still very much a case of take what you are given.

The Crossleys were another story! Following the war the corporation realised that major fleet requirements were necessary and, following Ministry of Transport guidelines, sought Ministry of Transport approval for sixty new double-deckers. These were to have been all Crossley DD42/3Ts with automatic turbo transmission. These were seen as a natural replacement for the successful Daimler fluid semi-automatics which, pre-war, the drivers had become used too. There were to be twelve high-bridge fifty-six-seat buses and forty-eight low-bridge fifty-three-seat vehicles for delivery by October 1947. In the event the Ministry of Transport loan finance was not made available and the total order reduced to thirty-six, to include the four Weymann high-bridge-bodied Bristols, Nos 88–91, which had been the first post-war non-austerity buses delivered to Luton in 1946. This delivery permitted the Crossley high-bridge order to be reduced to eight, at a cost of £1,595 for each chassis and £1,495 for each of the bodies.

Nos 92–94 were delivered late in 1946, the other five, Nos 95–99, in 1947. Regrettably, despite their initial popularity nationally, they were to prove unsuitable, as was found with a number of other municipalities. They were unreliable and had very heavy fuel consumption (up to thirty-five gallons a day), and they also tended to 'roll back' on hills when fully loaded! To conquer these problems, a few years later, in 1953, replacement AEC crash gearboxes and AEC 7.7-litre engines were fitted. This left an outstanding order of twenty-four low-bridge vehicles for delivery in 1947.

A letter was received from the Ministry of Transport concerning the loan application to meet the purchase of the remaining twenty-four buses. The necessity for their purchase was questioned,

49. Fleet No.84. Bristol K6A AEC 7.7 Park Royal.

50. Demonstration by Crossley.

in view of the 'general economic circumstances', and the council were asked to consider whether it was essential to embark on 'such expenditure'. The Ministry had originally given their approval to the relevant tenders on a 'without prejudice' basis. Ultimately, by December, the Ministry of Transport had agreed the loan, subject to delay for one year in order to economise on their capital expenditure. This fell in rather nicely with the delivery delays that were being experienced. However, it was decided that, should delivery be available before the loan monies, then LCT would temporarily lease the vehicles.

In January 1946 London Transport applied to carry local passengers within the borough. This was simply so that they could divert the 321 and 727 services via Cutenhoe Road for the return, enabling them to arrive at the standing in Park Square on the correct side of the road. This was granted in May. The demand at this time for works buses for Vauxhall Motors was placing the fleet under pressure. Workers needed buses between 8 a.m. and 9 a.m. and again from 4.30 p.m. to 6 p.m. The pressure was not relaxed until the increase in the use of cars in the early sixties. This extra demand twice a day often generated problems in the town during weekday afternoons. The metropolitan Traffic Commissioner wrote to LCT in mid-1946 expressing dissatisfaction with peak hour services to the airport. This had to be overcome by LCT, who approached LPTB asking them to increase service 364 at peak times as LCT were still unable to operate double-deck vehicles to Luton Airport due to the state of Eaton Green Road.

In July 1946 the four Weymann-bodied K6As arrived. Despite this, LCT was unable to meet a request for an improved service to Houghton Regis due to a lack of vehicles. It was identified that to meet future anticipated traffic the twenty-four new vehicles would be required by 1948, at a cost of £90,000, and a further eleven for 1949 at an estimated cost of £44,000. In December 1946 preliminary informal discussions about some mutual working to save costs between LCT and ENOC were suspended because of proposals for the nationalisation of ENOC.

Due to a delay in the delivery of uniform clothing for women conductors an order was placed with Leeds City Transport for fifty partly worn outfits comprising of tunics and skirts. Applications were made in March 1947 to extend service 1 from Pembroke Avenue to Hockwell Ring, a recently developed housing estate at Leagrave. ENOC opposed the application, submitting one of their own. At this time an application was also made by LCT to provide a new service from Williamson Street to Stopsley via Lea Road and Crawley Green Road, as well as an Ashcroft Road–Stopsley service, but again ENOC objected. On 1 April 1947 the salary of the chief inspector of LCT was increased from £315 P/A to £360 P/A.

The service of voluntary conductors recruited during the war was terminated from 1 April 1947. At this time the Chief Constable was expressing concern at the traffic congestion in Park Square, which was being used as a bus terminal by too many operators. As a result of his concern it was suggested that a site should be found in the town to be used as a central bus terminal.

The general manager of Lahore and District Transport from Jamaica visited Luton for a month's experience. Also, in August 1947, four high-bridge Crossleys arrived.

Tenders were invited for the sale of the Dennis Lance and six Daimlers to be broken for scrap or spares (Nos 28, 14, 18, 37, 43, 44 and ?). A number of route disagreements between LCT and ENOC prompted an informal meeting arranged by the Transport Commission in October 1947 with a view to co-ordinate proposed and existing services to Leagrave. As a result of this meeting it was mutually agreed to run services on equal terms on a ten minute basis. Each operator was to provide a twenty-minute service. A further agreement was that there would be a shared service from the town centre to Stopsley via the new BISF (Steel Houses) Housing Estate using Ashcroft Road. This arrangement would only be temporary, pending continued negotiations with a view toward coordination of this and other services.

Probably about the same time that they were taken over by AEC during May 1947, Crossley Motors adopted a forty-four-hour week. This, together with increased material costs, prompted a rise in the cost of each bus to £250 each. Deliveries of the twenty-four low-bridge vehicles scheduled for October 1947 were initially deferred until March 1948. It then seemed unlikely they would be received before 1949, so between August and November three low-bridge buses were diverted from Chesterfield Corporation, part of an order for thirty. LCT was desperate for vehicles to support the manufacturing commitment of the town. Unfortunately, these three buses, Nos 109, 110 and 111, were to Chesterfield's own specifications, and although fitted with low-ratio gears became very unpopular with crews, and were little used when others became available. These buses had crash gearboxes, which were temperamental in the hands of most drivers, many of whom were used to automatic turbo transmission.

51. Rather a mess when a tree collapsed on to LCT No.86 whilst on route 7.

52. Rear view of the same bus.

53. LCT 98 pre-delivery at factory.

54. Lower-deck interior of a Crossley high-bridge (this is not believed to be a picture of a Luton bus: possibly for Manchester Corporation, who have the same layout and style of dark red and gold-coloured upholstery).

55. Fleet No.96, a Crossley high-bridge 8.6, later in life.

56. Crossley fleet No.110. One of the Chesterfield low-bridge buses delivered in 1947.

Since 1939 there had been various applications of maroon/cream liveries, cream having replaced white. The colour maroon was not always standard, no doubt varying due to both quality and availability during the war. However, it did seem to become progressively lighter over the years. Some pre-war vehicles retained red oxide roof and domes but otherwise mirrored the general mixture of applications seen throughout the fleet. 1946–47 deliveries were maroon with cream lower window surrounds continuing up to the base of the upper-deck, broken by a maroon waistband. An experimental livery of an elaborate light brown and cream was undertaken on repaints of older vehicles in the summer of 1947. Personally, I am not aware of any coloured pictures showing this livery. Neither am I aware which vehicle or vehicles were painted in this manner. This would tie up with a post-war timetable of around the same period, describing the corporation buses as brown and cream, although we could speculate that this may have been because the so-called maroon had become so dubious that it may have been considered brown!

A problem that occurred during the war was the recognition that most railway bridges in the town were too low for high-bridge buses. Deliveries during the war and immediately afterwards included some high-bridge vehicles. Naturally considerable care had to be exercised to make sure that these buses were only used on certain routes, and even then did not stray when not operating stage work. I personally remember an incident in 1954 when a Crossley high-bridge, No.95, with its roof peeled off, rather like a sardine tin, was wedged under the railway bridge in Guilford Street. The bus was being driven 'out of service' by a fitter, clearly not as aware as service drivers that the high-bridge buses were confined to routes 1, 1A, 4, 7 and 52D. Each of these buses had a white plate with red writing above the windscreen in the driver's cab warning the driver of these restrictions.

As we know the Crossley order had been reduced initially to thirty-six, then to thirty-two. The eight high-bridge buses delivered by the end of 1947 left twenty-four outstanding. The diversion of the three Chesterfield low-bridge buses reduced this to twenty-one still on order. It was clear that Crossley were unable to fulfil this obligation in the short term. At the same time the corporation were desperate for replacements. In November 1946 Crossley told the corporation to look elsewhere if they could, which they did. They found that Leyland could supply twelve complete low-bridge vehicles, they claimed, within six months! Five months after placing the order with Leyland, in January 1947, the price had increased. By accepting the twelve Leylands this now reduced the outstanding Crossley order to nine.

In November 1947 the Ministry of Transport delayed permission to LCT to borrow £84,000. LCT was then also asking for a further £90,000, making £174,000 in total. LCT was asked by the Ministry of Transport to re-consider its request. As a result, in December they withdrew their request for the additional £90,000 and advised Crossley and Leyland that orders for more vehicles from each manufacturer were to be placed in abeyance.

After the war buses had been freed from control, but by then another situation had arisen, that of delivery time. The corporation had been allocated eight Bristols with AEC engines in 1944–46. It would naturally have been desirable to obtain more of these, but, as this was not possible, the corporation had to turn to another manufacturer.

For reasons already mentioned, it was decided that for new vehicles the corporation would standardise on two types, which could be delivered within a reasonable period. These were Crossley and Leyland. Between 1946 and 1948 thirty-two new buses were acquired (for fleet details see Appendix 1). Twenty-one of these arrived in 1948: nine Crossleys and twelve Leylands. It was later accepted that it would have been preferable to standardise on Leyland, who had better service facilities in London, but just as Crossley had difficulty supplying buses, so too did Leyland who could supply no more than twelve buses per year, so the order had to be spread anyway.

In January 1948 a fare increase was proposed. In the February the £84,000 loan was approved. During 1948 the corporation adopted yet another variation in their livery, this time with maroon all over except for cream bands beneath the windows and a cream waistband with a black lining.

The last of the early post-war orders was fulfilled by mid-1948 when the remaining nine low-bridge Crossleys entered service. These vehicles were to spend much of their working lives on routes 5 and 6, and were numbered 100–108. The twelve Leyland Titan PD2/1s, with fifty-three seats and low-bridge bodies, were delivered between April and June 1948. These had a livery of maroon and cream, with the upper-deck painted cream with a maroon band. All had chrome radiator surrounds, apart from, it is believed, maybe two. At least one was painted red. Maintenance schedules over the years changed to suit differing PD2/1s of this batch. Later in their lives some of this batch also received aluminium surrounds, interchanged with those from the 1953 batch of

57. LCT fleet No.89 Bristol K6A
AEC.7.7 with Weymann body at
the Skimpot terminus. Delivered in
1946.

58. Mechanic working possibly on
an AEC engine in a Bristol!

59. Low-bridge Crossley fleet No.107.

PD2/10s. One peculiarity was that 112 and 119 had beading below the lower-deck windows on the offside only, whereas 113/5/20/3 had such trim on both sides. Others had none at all – such was the quality control!

Following this delivery of the twelve new Leylands, the corporation de-licensed ten obsolete double-deckers and three single-deckers, and invited offers. Amongst these were the last petrol-engined buses which had been withdrawn in April 1948, probably Nos 14 and 21. This now meant that, for the first time, the licensed fleet comprised entirely of diesel-engined buses.

However, the new Leylands mark the real start of my interest. As a four year old in 1948 I remember seeing a 'new bus', which aroused my curiosity. It was one of these new 1948 Leyland Titans. These became a regular feature on my home route from Stopsley to the town centre, route 11. These buses were later regarded as very dependable workhorses. How I used to pester my dear late mother to sit in the lower saloon at the front so that I could either stand behind the driver, watching his every move, or simply peer over the bonnet near side mudguard as we trundled the familiar route.

My late father, aware of my interest in corporation buses, arranged for me to clamber 'all over' the fleet one Sunday morning in 1951 at the Park Street depot located in the former tram sheds. What I would give now to re-live that experience with a camera!

Although it was not foreseen at the time, the introduction of a non-standardised fleet would lead to many operating problems, increasing costs. The more Luton expanded the more valuable the longer-distance services became. LCT was still saddled with short-distance services, and ended March 1948 with a net loss of £11,649, compared with a profit of £8,371 the previous year. In 1949 the loss jumped to £35,568.

After the war LCT and ENOC had disputed obstinately, in the traffic courts of 1947, about their respective share of certain routes in Luton. It became very difficult for either company to organise suitable extensions or alterations to existing services. There were many new housing developments in Luton at this time for which both operators were competing. The Traffic Commissioners expressed strong dissatisfaction at their failure to co-operate with each other. As a result we know already that coordination discussions took place but were suspended in December 1946 when proposals were made for the nationalisation of the Tilling Group companies.

In July 1948 the first draft of a coordination agreement was examined, and the first meeting took place on 26 October. At this time a number of pre-war double-deck Daimlers were renovated. An experiment was carried out by equipping one of the rebuilt Daimler buses with new-type fluorescent lighting. At the time this was the only vehicle in the country so equipped. The chief engineer of the Ministry of Transport arranged to inspect the vehicle.

60. Typical crews posing with an inspector on the platform of a Crossley.

61. Leyland PD2/1 fleet No. 122 about to embark with a full load to Whipsnade Zoo. Pictured in Luton LMR station in 1947.

ENOC became nationalised, along with all other Tilling Group companies, with effect from August 1948, into the new British Transport Commission.

By mid-November 1948 trouble was being experienced with the turbo transmitters on the first batch of the Crossley buses. It was decided to contact other operators to gain knowledge from their experience. The Transport Committee witnessed local tests of fully loaded Crossley buses both with turbo and crash gearboxes. The chief engineer of Crossley attended to answer questions, after which it was decided to accept the remaining six Crossleys ready for delivery and fitted with turbo transmission. In December a lease was taken on office premises in Bute Street at a rental cost of £1,300 P/A. Also in December Leyland approached the corporation referring to the order in abeyance, asking when they required the twelve buses on order so that they could schedule production. LCT was unable to give a clear answer as the coordination of services being discussed could well affect the requirement from a time perspective.

Many new housing estates, both private and council, sprang up with the post-war expansion of Luton and Dunstable, with Hockwell Ring, Ramridge, Stopsley and Farley Hill being the principle areas. In November 1947 LCT extended the Stopsley route 11 to Rochester Avenue, as did ENOC with their route 52D. Both these extensions had been agreed pre-war, but had not been implemented because the roads had not been fully made up. This situation gave rise to applications from both ENOC and LCT for further extensions and new routes. LCT applied for route extensions to route 1 to Hockwell Ring, route 15 to Ashcroft Road and route 12 to Somerset Tavern. These were all disputed and refused. The outcome was two routes to be shared between LCT and ENOC: LCT route 1 and ENOC route 57 to Hockwell Ring, and a shared route 55 from Luton via Ramridge End to Stopsley.

The 1932 agreement meant that a number of these areas fell into ENOC territory. The Traffic Commissioners suggested a joint approach, that the two operators combine their activities over certain areas. A sub-committee was formed for ENOC and LCT to meet and report on the possibility of co-ordinating bus services throughout the borough. Long negotiations ensued, resulting in an agreement to set up Luton and District Transport as a co-ordinating body for the services of the area. This was ratified by both sides and sealed on 11 October 1948.

A fare revision had been submitted in early September 1948 but was refused on the grounds that it would be unfair, and not in the public interest, to impose wholesale increases at a time when the fare

62. Leyland PD2/1 on route 11 passing Stopsley Green.

63. Rear end of PD2/1 fleet No.119 at the depot. A reminder for me of that day when I was seven!

and route structure would be under review as a result of the proposed coordination plans. In view of the continued losses that LCT would clearly suffer, at least until an agreement was reached, the town clerk drew attention to the provisions of the Transport Act of 1947 whereby the council was allowed to dispose of the Corporation Transport undertaking. No further mention is made of this observation. The burden of working out the details was borne almost entirely of John Kershaw, the ENOC area traffic superintendent, with Ronald Rogers, now the LCT deputy manager. Applications by LCT to operate buses outside the borough, so as to enable the terms of the coordination agreement to work, were submitted in November 1948. Birch Bros objected. After a public enquiry on 9 December permission was granted to LCT to operate outside the borough, except for a part of the A6 between Bramingham Turn and Streatley and roads east of Sundon. Consent was subject to the condition that the corporation could only run buses on such roads as part of the coordination agreement.

The new LDT commenced on Sunday 2 January 1949, and lasted for twenty-one years. The first stage of service coordination came into effect on 18 September 1949. This produced a saving for LCT of six buses and fourteen crew. In February supervisory staff were co-ordinated with ENOC. Briefly, the coordination objectives were:

a) To introduce longer, cross-town services in Luton.
b) To eliminate unnecessary duplication of journeys.
c) To achieve common fare scales with inter-available tickets.
d) To extend into growth areas with better use of vehicles.
e) To share mileage and revenue on a 50 per cent basis, or as near as is feasible.

The area covered in the Luton and District coordination agreement was as follows:

Borough of Luton
Houghton Regis
Dunstable
Dunstable, West Street to Whipsnade Road
Dunstable Downs, Whipsnade Cross Roads and 'Zoo'
Watling Street north to 'Green Man'
Watling Street south to 'Empire Rubber Company'
Houghton Regis to Toddington corridor

Toddington village, including Westoning Road
Fancott
Chalton
Sundon Park and Sundon
Warden Hill, Streatley
A6 to Streatley Turn and village (restricted)
A505 to Offley Cross Roads

The initial stage involved mostly Luton borough, Dunstable and Houghton Regis. Surrounding village services were to be reviewed at the second stage. Phase one involved sharing the revenue 50 per cent each. Phase two was calculated on revenue and mileage, with an income of 50 per cent each.

The joint venture became a very successful undertaking. For the corporation it represented an annual saving of £35,000. There were further savings due to not having to replace buses, resulting in savings on loan charges. Twelve members of the London Transport Executive (LTE) visited and inspected the Corporation Transport depot on 15 September 1949.

It is a pity that this arrangement had not taken shape some years earlier, as LCT would likely have avoided considerable trading losses. However, by March 1953 the annual loss had grown to £74,029. Needless to say, there remained persistent criticism that ENOC had got the better deal. Despite these difficulties, the two undertakings worked closely together. They claimed to have no secrets from each other: the two traffic superintendents were linked by direct telephone.

Mr. J. Robinson, who joined UC in 1956 as general manager, commented that 'The men who drew up this agreement produced a perfectly worded charter for the travelling public'. The greatest benefit was the linking of cross-town services, and a reduction in the central terminal points. Fares were standardised and the fare money was pooled. The agreement laid down that each operator should work 50 per cent of the total mileage within the designated area for 50 per cent of the pooled fares. UC continued as the coordinating partner when, in 1952, the Midland area of ENOC was transferred to UC.

In March 1949 Crossley announced an increase in the price of vehicles ordered in abeyance. This was as a result of Crossley adopting a forty-four-hour week, plus an increase in the cost of materials. By April LCT had altered the specification, and the agreed loan of £84,000 was exceeded by £3,304. In June the term of the loan was extended from eight to ten years. The advertising agent

64. Leyland PD2/1 LCT 117 makes its way up toward Round Green on route 11.

Harry Squires was authorised to sell advertising space on the reverse of tickets. An Ultimate automatic ticket machine system was placed on trial in 1949, to replace the traditional ticket and punch system. Initially six machines were tried on a hire charge of £5 P/A each. The system was simple and effective, and was adopted in 1951, resulting in a reduction of ticket staff in the offices by three.

The corporation disposed of six buses in June 1949. These were fleet Nos 30, 31,34,36,38 and 39. In November of 1949 a meeting was held in Holborn Town Hall, in north London. This was as the result of the 1947 Transport Act, which included a proposal made by the British Transport Commission to hold a series of meetings with borough representatives of a number of authorities. LCT contacted Southend-on-Sea in order to find out what was involved. The meeting took place on 8 November. LCT objected to whatever proposals were made, and nothing more was heard on the matter. In November 1949 fleet No.15's engine and chassis were overhauled for use as a LCT mobile library.

ENOC asked LCT for temporary hire of six double-deck vehicles at a charge of £18 per week, plus insurance and licensing costs. ENOC were responsible for maintenance costs. I am aware that at least one bus was hired in this way, and could have been the one I saw in Bedford (referred to below), presumably due to a vehicle shortage. Also during 1949/50 ENOC crews on ENOC duties worked some LCT vehicles. This practice was adopted to balance the mileages, but was not continued for the future.

As a young lad I had grandparents in Bedford and often travelled the ENOC route to Bedford Station, at that time located near St Johns Church. I remember one evening, around 1949–50, arriving at the bus station with my parents to catch the ENOC bus home to Luton. To my surprise I saw a LCT vehicle on one of the stands. If my memory serves me correctly it was one of the low-bridge Crossleys indicating Dunstable on the blind. This would, of course, have been ENOC service 3. Whether it had been brought over on a Bedford run to supplement a shortage of ENOC vehicles, or mileage balancing, we will never know. Needless to say, there was an ENOC Bristol K5G to take us home to Luton.

As a result of the implementation of the second stage of the coordination agreement, major service changes occurred on 18 September 1949 and 16 September 1951. With the co-ordinated area now stretching to Great Offley, Whipsnade Zoo, Toddington, Sundon and Streatley, this allowed operation of LCT buses to quite a number of places previously prohibited.

The corporation's contribution in the formation of Luton & District Transport was almost the same as the 1939 route schedule, apart from an additional service 1A, which was really an extension of service 1 to one of the new housing areas at Hockwell Ring.

65. Leyland PD2/1 fleet No.114, later in its life. Pictured leaving the town centre stop on service 11 bound for Stopsley.

66. Former tram depot, the first LCT bus garage in Park Street, Luton.

The Coordination Agreement

ENOC's contribution comprised of:

1. Those to be amalgamated with corporation routes.

52D	Luton (Park Square)–Hart Lane–Stopsley (the same number continued to be used)
55	Luton (Park Square)–Crawley Road–Stopsley
56/A	Cutenhoe Road/Vauxhall Works–Limbury
57	Luton (LMR Station)–Leagrave
63	Luton (Alma Street)–Warren Road

2. Those which would continue to be operated by ENOC but which came, either partly or wholly, within the coordination agreement.

3	Whipsnade–Dunstable–Toddington–Bedford
3B	Dunstable–Tebworth–Toddington
12	Luton–Streatley Turn–Shefford
12A	Luton–Streatley–Pegsdon
14	Luton–Meppershall
14A	Luton–Pegsdon
16	Luton–Dunstable–Aylesbury
18	Luton–Dunstable–Leighton Buzzard–Wing (via Hockliffe)
18A	Luton–Dunstable–Leighton Buzzard
18B	Luton–Dunstable–Tilsworth–Leighton Buzzard Station
20	Luton–Ampthill–Bedford
20/A	Luton–Wilstead–Bedford
20B	Luton–Clophill–Pulloxhill
20D	Luton–Clophill–Flitwick
52	Luton–Hitchin–Baldock
52B	Luton–Stotfold
52D	Round Green–Chaul End Lane
53	Luton–Leagrave–Dunstable (LMS or Rifle Volunteer)
53A	Luton–Dunstable (Direct)(LMS or Rifle Volunteer)

53C   Luton–Dunstable (Hambling Place)
66   Luton–Dunstable–Bletchley

Services were re-arranged as follows, to be operated by LCT except where shown as a shared operation or ENOC only.

LDT 1 and 1A
        LC 1A   2 and 3 combined and extended to become:
        LDT 1   Cutenhoe Road–Seymour Ave.
        LDT 1A   Cutenhoe Road–Hockwell Ring

LDT 4   LC 4 and ENOC 55 services combined and extended to become:
        LDT 4   Skimpot–Luton (Park Square)–Stopsley (Green)

LDT 5, 6 and 7   Unchanged

LDT 8   LC 8 re-routed: Bradgers Hill Road–Farley Hill Estate (Whipperly Way)

LDT 9   LC 9   Re-routed: Russell Rise–Biscot Mill

LDT 11 and 11A   LC 11 and 11A linked with ENOC service 63, linked to run:
                       Warren Road–Luton (Bridge Street)–Stopsley (Rochester Ave)

LDT 12   LC 12 unchanged

LDT 13   Old LCT service 20

LDT 15   LC 15 withdrawn. Re-introduced as a works service Vauxhall–Farley Hill,
                       incorporating the former LCT 18 route

LDT 17   LC 17 unchanged

LDT 23 and 24   LC 23 and 24 unchanged

LDT 52D, LCT 21, 22 52D combined to run:
                       Shared operation LCT and ENOC 52D
                       Chaul End Lane–Hart Lane–Round Green–Stopsley–Vauxhall/Airport

LDT 53B   Luton–Dunstable–Whipsnade Zoo. A shared operation from September
                       1951, usually at weekends.

LDT 54   Luton–Toddington–Ampthill. LCT shared operation from 1951
                       onwards for those to Toddington only.

LDT 56, LCT 14 (LC 16 part transferred to ENOC later to run as LDT 14A) with ENOC 56 and 56A combined. ENOC operated but after September 1951 shared operation LCT and ENOC 56 from Park Square–Limbury (Biscot Mill)

LDT 57, LCT 13 and ENOC 57 combined to run:
                       (New LDT route 13, see LDT 20)
                       ENOC 57 Luton (LMR)–Leagrave (Hockwell Ring) ENOC oper-
                       ated but, after September 1951, a shared operation.

LDT 59 Luton–Sundon ENOC operated but, after September 1951, a shared operation.

6

DECADE OF CHANGE
1950–1959

A Repair and Maintenance Committee was established on 4 January 1950 to report on proposals to obtain temporary accommodation in which to establish a central repair and maintenance depot for the corporation. A report was also called for on the land forming part of the site of the former sewage pumping station, adjacent to the existing depot temporarily used for parking buses. The Ultimate ticket machines on trial were reported as working satisfactorily. As a result the rental period was extended.

Some fare anomalies were recognised within the co-ordinated area, to be removed as soon as possible. More frequent services were provided to the airport on Sundays, when 'joy rides and flying displays' took place. Some upset was caused when a petition from residents at Biscot Mill was received in June 1950. They asked for a restoration of the withdrawn service 14. It was reported that the petition arose because certain ENOC-operated runs on route 56 did not go to schedule. This

67. Ultimate ticket machine on trial. Introduced in 1950.

occurred at selected peak periods only when LCT increased the frequency on route 9. Meanwhile, the alternative ENOC route 56 was fully loaded. As a result ENOC agreed to operate according to the schedules, but, despite this, the council voted to try and secure a re-instatement of route 14.

Successful trials of the Ultimate ticket machines led to an agreement in September 1950 for the hire of twelve existing machines, plus a further forty-eight from Bell Punch Co. Ltd, for five years at £5 per machine. Following a move in August 1950 by ENOC for a fare increase on routes not covered by the coordination agreement. LCT applied in the September for an increase sufficient to generate an extra £20,000 P/A. This was put into effect on the last day of the year. As a result of an independent arbitration, award wages were increased with effect from 30 December. Drivers now received £5.15 and conductors £5.11 p/w.

Despite this award, in January 1951 the general manager reported extreme difficulty in maintaining scheduled services due to an acute shortage of drivers and conductors, and mentioned that if further deterioration occurred then services would have to be reduced. As a result a review of services was undertaken.

With continued growth in new housing, consideration was given to a proposal to extend the Farley Hill service 8 to Whipperly Way and service 9 to Priestleys/Longcroft Road. By 12 February 1951 a number of new employees had been taken on, but shortages still existed. In May an application was made to the Traffic Commissioners for revised services, under phase 2 of the coordination agreement. By the end of June the staffing was still only 84 per cent of the full compliment. Pressure was still coming from the Airport Committee for improved services, especially on Sundays and Bank Holidays. As a result, hourly stage services from Park Square in the town centre were agreed for a two-month experimental period, commencing 1 July. Four obsolete Daimlers, previously standing unused at the depot, were made available for sale and open to offers.

The end of year accounts for March 1951 were presented on 27 July when the council recommended that a special committee of seven councillors be appointed for the purpose of making a full enquiry into the administration and financial position of the transport undertaking. The accounts showed a net deficiency of around £60,000 at a time when there was a need for continued replacement of much of the fleet.

By the end of August it was clear from the figures that demand for the airport service during the two-month trial was minimal, except on 24 July when the Association of British Aero Clubs held an event. The licensing authority granted permission for revised services, under phase 2 of the coordination agreement, to commence on 16 September 1951. These changes also took into consideration increasing use of private cars, new housing developments and uneconomical services.

Following a recommendation from the special committee, formed in July, a report was commissioned in October from accountants Urwick Orr & Partners. Following the initial report on 31 January 1952 the council formally appointed them to undertake an investigation with the following terms of reference: 'To make an investigation into all branches of Luton Transport undertaking, to ascertain whether there is scope for securing further economies and an increase in efficiency.'

The report was prepared on the following basis:

> Admin and Control
> Traffic and Operations
> Engineering and Maintenance Policy

As a direct result of an earlier reduction in services, eight single-deck buses were now surplus to requirements. By November 1951, as a result of the increase in the number of employees at the airport, principally D. Napier & Sons Ltd, it was becoming increasingly difficult to meet demand at peak times.

In January 1952 two of the Crossleys were re-painted a brighter red, the same as the Leyland Titans. Although it had been withdrawn in 1952, No.27 was re-licensed during the year to help out on works duties, until finally being re-withdrawn in June.

On 3 January 1952 ENOC advised the corporation that the BTC had under consideration a scheme whereby, in respect of certain companies whose share capital was owned by them, there would be a re-arrangement of operating territories. Under the new scheme the Midland area of ENOC would be transferred to United Counties Omnibus Co. Ltd (UCOC). ENOC wanted to

68. Leyland PD2/1 LCT fleet No. 119 on route 4.

69. Leyland PD2/1 fleet No. 115 at Vauxhall Motors for a works service extension for route 1A.

70. Low-bridge Crossley (Chesterfield type) on works duty at Vauxhall Motors.

71. A brilliant bus picture capturing the period 1951 at Vauxhall Motors, and although mainly ENOC vehicles, LCT fleet No. 51 is in the foreground. Note the rear window and blind box on this Daimler COG5 Willowbrook. An earlier Daimler, probably a CH6 Willowbrook of 1933/34 vintage, draws away from the stand.

72. One of a series of pictures taken around 1951 at Vauxhall Motors. Note the blanked-out top rear window on the utility bus, the rear display on the Daimler in the foreground and the Leyland TD7 on the stand.

73. One of the Leyland TD7s pulls away from Vauxhall Motors on works duty.

know whether there would be any objections if UCOC entered into a supplementary agreement to help perform the obligations of the coordination agreement. The corporation accepted these proposals. Peak time problems at the airport continued to get worse as the workforce now expanded at English Electric. The eight single-deckers were sold for £187.10 each. Three further double-deckers were now available for disposal.

Quotations were received for the supply of five chassis and bodies for delivery in 1952. As a result five low-bridge, double-deck, 7ft 6in wide Leylands with synchromesh transmission, at a total cost of £19,000, were ordered, and an application made to the Ministry of Transport for the full sum. By the end of February this cost was to rise to £20,840. In an effort to resolve the peak problems, LCT approached the airport representatives suggesting that Napier and English Electric should stagger working hours. This suggestion was rejected, so the corporation then offered to hire out buses, provided Napier and EE covered the costs. They in turn rejected this suggestion.

A proposed extension of service 9 to Meyrick Avenue was rejected as roads were deemed unsuitable. The traffic manager agreed to look at any alternative way in which an improved service could be provided on this route. Messrs Urrwick Orr & Partners commenced their investigation on 31 March 1952. Approval was received on 18 April for an 11/2d maximum fare increase within the co-ordinated area.

Due to the impasse between the airport companies and the corporation, Napier & Sons Ltd applied to the licensing authority to operate their own stage bus service between the airport and Park Square at works times from Monday to Friday. Thankfully for the corporation the application was refused on the basis that it was in the general interest of all concerned that a transport undertaking operated stage services. LCT re-affirmed their willingness to hire vehicles and operate at Napier's and English Electric's expense, but there was no response. The recent application for a fare increase was agreed at the end of May. Seamarks, a local coach hire operator, applied to the licensing authority to operate a feeder service between Ampthill and Luton for their coach trips from Luton.

At the end of June 1952 LCT confirmed that the five new Leylands on order should be fifty-five-seat vehicles, and resolved that Leyland engines would power all future double-deck buses, be low-bridge, all-metal bodied and have synchromesh gears.

By early September 1952 the staffing position was again acute, down to 87 per cent of its full complement. The Seamarks application was agreed by the licensing authority, and was not objected

74. One of the Leyland TD7s fleet Nos 71-74 waiting at Vauxhall on a works service, probably bound for Round Green.

75. Another scene at Vauxhall Motors, *c.*1950.

to by LCT or ENOC provided it was operated on Sundays only. Back at the airport, Napier lodged an appeal to the Ministry of Transport. A further increase in fares was sought, but this time became subject to a public enquiry.

Leyland was advised that route destination blinds on the five new buses ordered should be visible from the rear instead of the nearside. These vehicles were to be painted in a brighter red than those currently in service.

On 11 September 1952 sections 1–7 of the accountant's report became available, in which it was stated that in the consultant's opinion they were unable to find that the management of the under-taking could be held responsible for the worsening financial situation, and that the main value of the investigation should prove to be the removal of this misapprehension that exists amongst the public and the rate payers.

A copy was sent to the licensing authority in support of the recent application to increase fares. At the time of the report the fleet comprised of sixty-three double-decks, where a maximum of fifty were used at peak periods. The report was critical of the fleet composition, which was varied. The councillors recognized that future standardisation would be a good thing. They recognised how this varied chassis situation came about, as until the outbreak of war all vehicles were built on Daimler chassis. During and immediately after the war the Ministry of War Transport allocated vehicles under licence. Operators were not free to choose as they wished. In spite of restrictions the corporation realised that they had been fortunate in obtaining four of the forty buses Leyland were permitted to produce in 1942. During the year seats from redundant Daimlers were re-fitted to the Bristol auster-ity buses, replacing their wooden seats. It was realised that repainting the buses with cream outlines meant more time off the road, and consequently it was decided that all future repaints would be 'all red' with a single cream waistband, as would all new deliveries.

Discussions took place in October 1952 to extend service 8 at the Farley Hill end of the route. The general manager reported that he had a meeting with UCOC to operate an experimental stage shuttle service between the town centre (George Street) and Farley Hill estate at peak traffic peri-ods. This was implemented on 24 November 1952, on a Monday to Friday basis.

The Ministry of Transport held a hearing on 10 October 1952 regarding the appeal by Napier over the airport issue. With effect from 9 November 1952, service 4 would operate along a new section of Ashcroft Road, instead of Williton Road and Yeovil Road. The licensing authority agreed on an increase in the fare structure with effect from 2 November. During the year the last remaining Daimler single-decker, No.27, was formally withdrawn from service, but seems to have retained its PSV licence as there are reports of its continued use on stage service and school runs up until early 1953 when it was cut down and retained as a tow vehicle. My own recollection of the Daimlers was naturally during their latter years. Around 1951 both single and double-deckers had been relegated to lighter duties such as school specials and works relief. I remember they certainly used to rattle an awful lot, or perhaps it was just the noise of all of us children on the school buses during the early fifties! By 1952 there were only eleven pre-war vehicles in the fleet acquired during the years 1936–38.

On 1 December 1952 an agreement was reached regarding the conversion of the turbo Crossleys. These had been found unsatisfactory due to heavy fuel consumption and unreliability. AEC Sales Ltd agreed to convert seventeen vehicles by fitting new orthodox synchromesh gearboxes to the 7.7 engines, at a cost of £485 each. The work was to be undertaken at their Southall repair depot. As usual LCT borrowed the money (£8,245 over five years) to meet the cost. Two vehicles were delivered to Southall in the first instance, and when another vehicle was collected a further one was delivered. The work took around two weeks for each bus. A further and somewhat irritating problem with these high-bridge Crossleys were the loose windows. These had a mind of their own, much to the discomfort of the passengers, and opened on whim.

At this time staff shortages had been more or less alleviated, fallen to within 8 per cent of the full complement. The outcome of the airport appeal hearing was a dismissal. Much to the annoyance of English Electric and Napier, LCT had meanwhile hired vehicles from Seamarks Bros to provide relief on the basis that Napier would meet any shortfall between hire charges and the fares collected, which to them seemed a reasonable solution.

Luton Road Safety Committee approached the undertaking to consider the proposal that all new buses should have auto-operated doors. The request was simply noted.

In January 1953 it was decided to purchase a spare Leyland engine to make possible the commencement of a maintenance programme for the fleet on a unit replacement basis. Although it was agreed that this arrangement would be adopted, it was decided to defer the purchase until all the Leylands currently on order were received. The earlier order for five buses had meanwhile been increased to ten. Quotations were at the same time sought for five further Leyland 7ft 6in bodied, double-deck, low-bridge buses fitted with synchromesh gearboxes. These were subsequently ordered on 2 March 1953, at a cost of £4,100 each. A further loan from the Ministry of Transport for £20,500 was sought, which would make possible a total order of fifteen buses of this type.

The coronation of Queen Elizabeth II was to take place in June 1953. To celebrate an illuminated bus would tour the town for a week. Arrangements were made for the conversion of a single-deck bus. Luton College of Further Education was asked to invite students from the art department to submit designs for the bus.

The staff shortage problem had returned by March 1953, and was down 13 per cent on the full complement. By May 1953 this shortfall had risen again to 17 per cent.

In May 1953 there were three proposed service changes: service 7 was to terminate at Biscot Mill instead of Fountains Road, service 8, an hourly service between Bridge Street and Russell Rise, was to be amended and made more frequent, and service 9 was to operate at a twenty-minute frequency between Biscot Mill and Longcroft Road – all these to be effective from 1 November. In view of the number of protests, and although agreed by the licensing authority, permission was withdrawn on 1 October 1953. A public meeting was arranged and permission finally granted on 20 October allowing the amended services to commence on 1 November. This introduction reduced pressure on service 8 from Priestley at peak periods.

In June 1953 four Daimler double-deck buses became available for disposal (61, 62, 63 and 66), and these were sold to the Benhill Machinery & Equipment Co. in London. On 23 June there was a visit by twelve members of the LTE, who were given a tour of the depot followed by tea in the staff canteen. At the September council meeting a presentation was given to Mr R.G. Smith of an engraved testimonial demonstrating the council's appreciation of his thirty years in service as a driver both with the corporation and their predecessor on the trams.

Unlike many other operators at the time smoking had not been banned in the lower saloon, only a request asking passengers to refrain. This was seen as acceptable due to the difficulty in enforcing prohibition rules.

76. High-bridge Crossley fleet No.93 on route 1A at Park Square.

Thirteen years after the war the council were invited to submit a compensation claim for war damage under the War Damage Act of 1943 in respect of that part of the depot which had been completely destroyed by enemy bombs on 22 September 1940.

It was considered that although the variety and types of buses purchased in recent years were largely outside the control of the council, there were decisions which in hindsight were unfortunate. Namely the decision to acquire sixteen high-bridge bodies during 1944–47, and the decision to have turbo transmitters fitted to the seventeen new Crossley buses. The high-bridge buses added fleet operating difficulties, being limited to certain routes in a town centre with many low bridges. You will recall that, since 1952, the policy was to purchase only low-bridge bodies.

In 1953 the undertaking received the first batch of ten Leyland PD2/10s, the remaining five being delivered in 1954. These all had more substantial Leyland Farington bodies, with an enhanced level of trim. By April 1953 the livery of the latter years began to appear: pillar box red, with one cream band above the lower-deck windows. Initially five of the new buses were given a cream upper-deck surround: these were of the 1953 delivery, fleet Nos 124–128. With the completion of the PD2/10 delivery in 1954, withdrawal of the last pre-war vehicles was possible. It would be a further three years before withdrawals would enable the fleet to comprise solely of post-war vehicles.

I always felt that these PD2/10s, together with the later PD2/30s delivered in 1960 with Weymann/East Lancs. bodywork, were the best vehicles in the fleet. These PD2/10s were amongst the last vehicles that were all Leyland built. Leyland ceased body building in 1953, although the last five were not completed and delivered until 1954. The big downside of these PD/2/10s was, however, the sliding windows. These quickly became loose and had the habit of sliding open/closed when going downhill and visa-versa uphill, making it a bit draughty on a cold day!

At the end of 1953 a further eight obsolete buses were sold (58, 64, 66, 76, 77, 78 and 79) to Billy Smart's Circus, and 82 to J. Carney of Rugeley. In April 1954 crew numbers remained 14 per cent below a full complement. An application by the Omnibus Society requesting a tour of routes and a visit to the depot during July, on a Saturday, was agreed. During the previous three years experiments had taken place with a suppressor, which would practically eliminate interference on televisions from windscreen wipers on the buses. The suppressor would be fitted to all vehicles by the following September. Further obsolete buses 51, 53, 70, 71, 72 and 73 were sold to Birds Commercial Motors of Stratford-upon-Avon. A 1939 Fordson 25cwt van (FYW 479) was sold locally to a Mr Anderson. By September the crew deficiency had risen to 22 per cent below strength, and was now at a seriously low level.

Quotations for nine more buses were sought from Leyland, five for delivery in 1955 and four in 1956. Leyland subsequently advised that they had ceased to build the coachwork, and that the quotation was based upon coachwork supplied by MCW Ltd. LCT decided to invite tenders for coachwork by public advertisement, as for some reason they were not keen on MCW bodies.

At the end of the year crews were back to 16 per cent below strength, with 161 platform staff.

Due to the condition of Eaton Green Road the airport service 23 was re-routed via Crawley Green Road and Eaton Valley Road, with effect from 5 November 1954. On 1 December 1954 a high-bridge bus, No.95, being driven by a fitter on a test run, had its roof severely damaged under a railway bridge in Guilford Street. The incident is mentioned in the last chapter, and was personally witnessed by me as I was on a No.11 bus which had to be diverted along Mill Street and Manchester Street, which meant that we alighted in the centre of the town, facing in the wrong direction. To continue its route, this No.11 bus had to go up Alma Street.

Following a review, a committee had been set up in the October of 1954 to look into wages and conditions of service. The committee reported that, in general, both wages and conditions were better than those of most other municipal undertakings. Nevertheless, as an industrial town, wages of the major seven manufacturers, amongst them Electrolux, SKF, Commer and Vauxhall, remained the principle stumbling block to obtaining and retaining staff.

In January 1955 crews were 18 per cent short of a full complement. In view of the continuing problems with staff, but in the light of the report by the Review Committee, lengthy consideration was given to introducing (1) a bonus scheme based upon (a) increased revenue (b) length of service and efficiency and (c) timekeeping or commission on fares collected, or both, and (2) the provision of housing accommodation either from council general allocation, subsidised housing or by building houses without subsidy. Eventually it was considered best to give a reasonable increase in basic rates of pay, as it was felt that this would attract sufficient additional employees and cause an overall saving, set against the alternatives proposed which would likely involve considerable overtime being worked.

Seven tenders were received for coachwork for the Leyland order. The contract was, after all, placed with MCW, subject to agreement on specification. If unsuitable then the Park Royal tender would be accepted, as both were asking for £11,100 for five bodies. The chassis were quoted at £10,353.18.9. An application for a loan for the total of £21,454 was applied for from the Ministry of Transport. Deputy Transport General Manager Mr R. Rogers resigned on 28 February 1955 as a result of his successful application for the post of deputy transport general manager with

77. Fleet No.128 Leyland PD2/10 Farington, in its 1953 delivery colours.

Southend on Sea Corporation Transport. Applications were invited for a replacement by public advertisement. At this time crew numbers were still around 18 per cent below a full complement.

The general manager reported that it would probably be necessary to increase the fleet numbers in the not too distant future, and that the present depot would be inadequate. Sub-depots, or out-station garages, were considered inappropriate, so it was decided to look for a suitable site in the vicinity of Chaul End, midway between Luton and Dunstable. After consideration this was seen as an unsuitable option. Meanwhile discussions were taking place with UCOC with regard to an extension of existing services, which would be necessary to meet future needs as a result of industrial and residential growth within the co-ordinated area. The general manager submitted for consideration a report on the merits and disadvantages of sub-depots as against the replacement of the existing depot by a new depot in another location.

Wages remained a problem; despite the corporation's willingness to agree an increase for drivers and conductors, they were precluded from doing so by the Federation of Municipal Passenger Transport Employees (FMPTE) who held that the corporation's review of wages and conditions was outside the terms and objects, constitution and procedure of the NJIC for the road passenger transport industry which provided that any agreement relating to such matters should be agreed nationally. They also contended that bonus schemes were just as contrary to the decisions of the NJIC as alterations in basic rates of pay. They were of the opinion that, in keeping with statistics obtained from other operators, increased wages would not ease the staff shortages, and that they could not agree with the introduction of differential basic rates of pay on an area or district basis. Crews were now operating only 10 per cent below strength, which was certainly an improvement despite there being no material increase in wages and conditions.

In June 1955 Leyland reported that delivery of the five chassis would be delayed. In September an order for four more Leyland chassis costing £8,963 was placed, together with an order for bodies with MCW to replace four buses scheduled to become obsolete in November 1956. Some concern at the current delay of the Leyland order was expressed.

In an effort to improve the staffing situation the corporation approached the FMPTE to gain permission for a bonus scheme on top of nationally agreed rates of basic pay, provided the bonus scheme was approved by FMPTE. By the end of September staff levels were within 9 per cent of a full complement. The FMPTE eventually agreed that a bonus of £9 6s per week could be paid, to be known as a deviation payment.

78. Leyland PD2/10 fleet No. 129 fairly early in its life, illustrated by a hand-painted Bovril advert, following a re-paint without the upper-deck cream window surround and with cream lower-deck waistband on the sides.

79. Leyland PD2/10 fleet No.128 later in its life with the then regular livery of pillar box red with single cream band above the lower-deck.

80. Leyland PD2/10 fleet No.131.

A suggestion was made at the borough council meeting on 1 September 1955 that a film be made of the transport undertaking, as Sunderland Corporation had done. However, it was revealed that the Sunderland film was concerned with trams and not buses, so, sadly, the idea died at that point and no further action was taken. On 1 December 1955 the local paper *Luton News* asked the general manager to write an article for publication in its industrial supplement on the subject of public transport in the Luton area. The government introduced a fuel oil tax at the end of 1955, creating another increase in cost.

Not surprisingly, in January 1956 a fare revision was sought, ostensibly to defray the cost of a national pay award. Crew numbers were still 9 per cent below a full complement, and no improvement had occurred since the national pay award. It was considered that a local variation, by way of a bonus scheme, would, on reflection, not solve the staff shortage problem unless the incentive offered was so significant as to render it impracticable and uneconomic. Members of the Co-ordinated Transport Committee were invited by UCOC to tour their Northampton depot on 21 March 1956. Arrangements were agreed for twelve members of LTE to tour LCT's depot in July 1956. Leyland advised the corporation that, as a result of a concentration of production on priority export orders, it was unlikely that the five new buses on order would be received before November 1956. In late March the licensing authority arranged a public enquiry in Luton to take place on 13 April in respect of the application by Luton District Transport for a fare increase. Following the inquiry the increase was approved and implemented on 20 May 1956.

In August 1956 crews were still 9 per cent below a full complement. Following a submission by residents, consideration was given to an extension of service 9 to Bradgers Hill Road. As with similar requests for other routes the suggestion was declined due to the perceived shortage of vehicles and crews.

On 27 September 1956 one new Leyland bus was delivered with three more expected within two weeks. This must have been a relief. These were the Leyland PD2/22s with MCW bodies of the lightweight Orion all-metal body type. They were the usual half-cab unit, but with full-width panel fronts. The design of Midland Red origin, with no external radiator, was very austere, and there was nothing appealing about these vehicles. They rattled a lot, and were to become most unpopular with both crews and passengers, often referred to by the former as 'a mass of shimmering tin'.

It was decided that at some stage it would be beneficial to link service 9 with 23 (Airport–Park Square) and extend to Bradgers Hill Road. This is believed to have been achieved in February 1958 as service 9. In November 1956 crew numbers had improved to within 5 per cent of the full complement.

The introduction of petrol/oil rationing forced a 5 per cent cut on public transport operators, to be introduced from 17 December. Talks were immediately held with UCOC to establish the effect on co-ordinated services. Six buses were disposed of in November (Nos 80, 81, 84, 85, 86 and 87).

With effect from 1 January 1957 fuel costs increased by 1s 5d per gallon, 1s of which was excise duty. Under an Act of Parliament p.s.v. operators could charge fares in excess of those permitted by conditions imposed by their licence, but only to cover the temporary increase in fuel costs, judged to be no more than one-twelfth of their normal receipts. LCT decided that all 2d fares be increased to 2½d. Additional revenue amounting to £10,000 per annum would, in any event, be less than the total increase in fuel costs.

Early in 1957 the first Leyland PD2/31 was delivered, still with the austere MCW all-metal body. On 3 January crews were only 1 per cent below the full complement of 194. An application was made for changes to service 9, as mentioned earlier. In March the Transport Committee resolved that smoking should be prohibited on lower-decks, and that UCOC should be asked to co-operate by imposing a similar prohibition in respect of their double-deck buses operating in the co-ordinated area. This was agreed by UCOC to be implemented at a date to be arranged. MCW submitted their outstanding account for the supply of nine bodies. The account was in excess of the quote by £1,435.56d, which they claimed was due to increases in the costs of labour and materials, given the delay in receiving the appropriate chassis from Leyland.

A strike by UCOC in the late summer caused a loss to the pooled revenue. As a result LCT sought a meeting with a view to coming to an equitable arrangement, which was agreed on a pro rata basis. A national pay award imposing an estimated additional cost of £10,000 P/A prompted yet another request for a fare revision on 28 October. The increase was discussed. Tenders were invited from Leyland for five more chassis for delivery during 1958.

81. Leyland PD2/10 fleet No. 126 was, I believe, the only one of the batch to have opening top front ventilators.

On 2 January 1958 Seamarks and W. & E.F. Kershaw Ltd sought a licence to operate stage services from Alma Street (outside the Cresta Ballroom) to various parts of Luton throughout the year at midnight and on occasions when late functions were held. LCT and UCOC objected, but agreed provided that adequate protection of their interest as stage operators in the area was otherwise protected. No doubt encouraged by their success, Seamarks applied for licences to operate tour feeder services to Luton at times when they were operating tour services from Luton under existing licences. Again LCT and UCOC objected, but later withdrew the objection provided that their stage operations were otherwise protected. Three obsolete buses were disposed of to G.H. Groves & Son Ltd.

Wages continued to be an issue. During January the FMPTE enquired of LCT whether they wished to continue to pay their crews the bonus agreed at 9s 6d per week. LCT responded that they wished to continue. Thankfully the NJIC approved the council's application to continue the deviation payment at the same rate. The National Council would automatically review the matter the next time a national award was made. As a result of a surfeit of claims in recent years the Municipal Mutual Insurance Co. Ltd sought a substantial increase in premium. Tenders were invited from twenty-two other insurers, but no lower quote was received. A premium of £4,357.12.5d was grudgingly accepted.

The final account from MCW representing five bus bodies was £1,084.16.8d in excess of the original tender/quote. Increases in labour and material costs were blamed. In late March 1958 six tenders for five more double-deck buses were invited for fitting to Leyland the chassis for which an order had been placed. These were scheduled for delivery in autumn 1958. The MCW tender was accepted although it was only the fourth lowest. A loan of £23,731 was agreed by the Ministry of Transport. Weekly receipts for corporation buses had risen to £7,349 by May 1958. Crews remained almost at full complement.

In September 1958 the borough council agreed that future buses ordered would be of 8ft width as opposed to 7ft 6in. To increase the width of five chassis on order from Leyland would cost a further £52 per chassis, but no increase in cost of bodies by MCW. The go ahead was therefore given. In October 1958 the general manager submitted a schedule of fleet replacements likely necessary in 1961, 1962 and 1963. He maintained that during this period thirty-six vehicles would likely be required. He explained that those purchased between 1946 and 1948 would be due for replacement. He suggested that the life of some of these vehicles should be adjusted to ensure that the replacement programme ran over a five-year period. These suggestions were implemented.

A full complement of crews was achieved in October 1958 at 202. A national pay award on 26 October was approved by the NJIC, but, as far as LCT was concerned, the award was made on the basis that the deviation payment, hitherto 9s 6d, was reduced to 8s, conditional upon the operation of a working schedule of forty-eight hours per week. For the first time in eleven years LCT was solvent. At the end of 1958 there remained a balance sheet surplus of £1,676, but with no reserves.

In common with good business practice it was considered appropriate that any future surplus, after costs and repayment of debts, should be placed in reserve to create a fund for replacement buses with a view to obliterating the need to continually borrow. It was hoped that this could be achieved over a fifteen-year term. Saturday night late services from the town centre started on 10 January 1959, and would run during the winter months. In February 1959 the NJIC reviewed the deviation payment rates, which were at that time 8s per week, and an agreement was reached to continue at the same level until a further review in twelve months. There was commendation by the borough council as to the manner in which the crews had maintained services during a particularly bad period of winter weather. By early 1959 the fleet numbered sixty-five buses, mainly Crossleys and Leylands. In March 1959 a further batch of five Leylands were delivered, this time PD2/30s with MCW bodies.

By 1959 there were thirty-two routes in the co-ordinated area. One of the most outstanding features of the coordination agreement had been the success of the cross-town services, which had been linking various routes thereby avoiding terminus congestion in the town centre. Probably the most successful of these routes were Nos 11 and 4. Services which had previously only operated at factory start and finish times grew into regular services, often serving new housing estates. The biggest employer was Vauxhall Motors whose pay roll rose from 12,000 in 1949 to 22,000 by 1959. 4,000 of these worked at Dunstable.

In May 1959 the LTE advised LCT of their application to the Traffic Commissioner to charge local fares within the borough of Luton on services 321, 321A and 326. By virtue of section 15 of the Transport Act of 1933, they did not, however, intend seeking authority to do likewise over stretches of the Farley Hill routes. Needless to say, both LCT and UCOC sought to protect their interests and complained to LTE to withdraw their application.

In June 1959 the borough council met with UCOC regarding the then proposed omnibus station in an area bound by Bridge Street, Guilford Street and Wilkinson Street, to be jointly managed and financed within the terms of the co-ordinated agreement. The crew numbers had remained marginally below the full complement for some while and were, in June 1959, at 3 per cent below

82. Fleet No.147 Leyland PD2/22 MCW emerging into New Bedford Road as it approaches the town centre.

83. Fleet No.142 Leyland PD2/22 MCW pictured early in its life with pillar box red and cream lining out of part lower and upper-deck windows. Seen heading toward Park Square from the depot.

optimum level with an actual crew staff of 207. Extension of the heavily used service 4 at the Stopsley terminus to Crowland Road was proposed but not yet implemented.

Information concerning a new type of low-deck bus with a front entrance and a seating capacity of sixty-two was disclosed to the council. Following the initial success of the Bristol Lodeka, with British Transport, Dennis subsidiaries had reached an agreement in 1957 to build their version of this arrangement which would be available to the municipal and private operators. An initial quote was obtained of £2,975 for the chassis and £2,993 for the bodywork. These vehicles were to be fitted with the usual Leyland engines on this 'Bristol type' chassis, manufactured under licence by Dennis Bros of Guilford, with bodies by East Lancs. Coachbuilders. The cost of these buses was approximately £1,100 more than the traditional fifty-five-seat bus normally purchased by LCT.

The general manager was authorised to obtain quotes for five more chassis from Leyland. Six quotations were received for five new bodies for normal fifty-five-seat buses. East Lancs. was chosen and although they offered the second lowest quote, at a cost of £11,975, these bodies were to a higher specification, and were particularly fine vehicles, solid and of pleasing design and finish. They were to be the last rear-entrance buses delivered to the corporation. Other quotes were received for two low-deck buses, at a chassis cost of £5,950 and a body cost of £5,986. These were all accepted, and a loan of £35,904 was sought from the Ministry of Transport. These two buses had the new low-deck Dennis chassis with Leyland engines and East Lancs. bodies.

Negotiations were concluded in September 1959 'subject to contract' with Vauxhall Motors who were interested in the purchase of fourteen acres of land, including the existing transport depot, former fire station garage, former sewage pumping station and temporary public slaughterhouse, for £180,000. This would enable a suitable alternative site for a new transport depot to be obtained. This was agreed on the basis that the transport undertaking would not have to bear a financial burden greater than that which, in the ordinary course of events, arose in the next five years due to the extension and improvement of the present depot set against the erection of a replacement garage on another site. In other words, if the sale went ahead LCT would be in no worse a financial position than if it had not gone ahead.

Along with the proposed extension of service 4 to Stopsley, an extension to the other heavily used service 11 was proposed at the Stopsley terminus to Wandon Close. A licence for this extension was applied for in November 1959. Typical LCT revenue receipts for a week in October 1959 were £7,769. Crew staffing at 207 was still at 3 per cent below the full complement.

84. Fleet No.148 Leyland PD2/31 MCW outside the Town Hall.

85. Leyland PD2/31 MCW fleet No.155 with upper front vents.

In November 1959 the purchase of properties in Guilford Street commenced as preparations began to establish the town's first bus station. Plans for the new transport depot were also moving ahead. It had been decided to purchase eleven acres of land, buildings (including ten cottages in Kingsway, midway between Luton and Dunstable), at a total cost of £85,000.

The annual review of the deviation payment by the NJIC was due in February 1960. LCT submitted that the 8s payment should not be reduced while a forthcoming wage increase was being considered by the NJIC for the industry. Plans for the new bus station in the town centre were approved. It was agreed that, when complete, the new transport depot in Kingsway would be placed under the control of the LCT, although it would house other corporation vehicles as well as buses.

7

THE FINAL YEARS
1960–1970

In 1960 new council housing estates were begun at Lewsey Farm and Houghton Regis, which would attract an additional 30,000 people to the town between 1960 and 1965.

Problems had arisen with the proposed extension of service 11 so a public enquiry was scheduled for 4 February 1960. Any objections were overruled and, following the enquiry, permission was granted. One report shows that this extension was implemented in May 1960, another in October 1961.

The two Dennis Loline 11s with East Lancs. bodies were delivered in 1960. These were the first front-entrance double-deckers to enter the fleet. No.164 had been exhibited on the Dennis stand at the commercial motor show at Earls Court, fitted with chrome wheel trims especially for the show, which were later removed prior to delivery. These were actually regarded as an experimental order as they were not only front entrance but also Loline, a design pioneered by the Bristol Lodeka (Eastern Coach Works, ECW). LCT had always had to rely mainly upon low-bridge bodywork. The disadvantage to passengers of such vehicles is well known: the Loline buses introduced additional headroom. The success of these experimental vehicles heralded the style to be ordered for the next five years, over which period a further twenty-two front-entrance Loline double-deckers were delivered, with chassis by Albion and Dennis.

In March 1960 the NJIC agreed to deviation pay rates but reduced the payment to 7s for a forty-two hour week. This had been introduced by the FMPTE as a result of recommendations by the Wages Commission (a government body). These arrangements would result in estimated extra costs of £2,700 P/A. Consequently another fare revision was sought. The general manager reported that the revised forty-two-hour working week would come into effect on 28 March. Many alterations in service schedules were necessary to meet the new requirements. This was not only due to changes in the crew schedules but to the forty-two-hour week, as applied to the engineering industry generally. Many local factories had to change their working patterns. Therefore, a considerable liaison took place between LDT and local employers to determine the demand for different timetables. In all the changes were handled well and responded to positively by the crews. In May 1960 both services 4 and 11 were extended as previously proposed. The earlier fare revision was approved and implemented on 28 August 1960.

By late June 1960 it became clear that the five new buses that were due from East Lancs. would be delayed. As a result, five of the Crossleys were re-seated. Plans for the Kingsway depot were finalised and the contract put out to tender. At this time typical weekly revenue for LCT was £8,410 p/w. Crew numbers were actually in excess of basic requirement of 222 by two. With the natural expansion of housing estates in Dunstable it was realised that on certain services over certain roads within Dunstable borough it was necessary to formalise supplementary agreements to the original co-ordinated agreement of 1948, to ratify the current situation.

86. Leyland PD2/30 East Lancs. fleet No.158. Delivered in 1960, these had a more substantial body with a higher standard of trim, rather more like the earlier Farington PD2/10s.

87. Leyland PD2/30 East Lancs. fleet No.162. This was the last rear-entrance bus delivered to LCT.

LTEs visited the depot on 5 September and were, as usual, given tea in the staff canteen. The Southern Counties Touring Society sought a visit, and LCT agreed to provide a free tour in a Dennis Loline and put on afternoon tea. A brief glimpse of the tour in the Dennis Loline is shown on a video entitled *Omnibus UK Archive 2*, available from Reel Time Films Ltd.

Given the initial success of the two Dennis Loline fleet Nos 163 and 164, which they bought on a trial basis in 1960, it was the corporation's intention to order more of this type. An order was placed in early February 1961 for six more chassis fitted with Leyland engines, at a cost of £3,310 each. However, this order was to be frustrated. Meanwhile, the usual full loan was sought from the Ministry of Transport, and quotations were sought for six sixty-four-seat front-entrance bodies.

The annual review of the bonus deviation rate was continued at 7s for another twelve months. The compulsory purchase of properties around the area of the proposed new central bus station in the town centre continued. In 1961 the salary of the deputy transport manager was £1,650 P/A. This would have been good money at the time, probably equivalent to a bank manager of a large branch. The Ministry of Transport dismissed an appeal by Dunstable Borough Council to with-hold permission for stage operations covering local roads in the borough. On 10 August a fare revision was sought in view of the general increase in costs. This was granted and implemented on 15 October. Crew staffing at the end of August was in excess of the full complement of 224 with a staff of 228. Dennis Bros informed the corporation of an increase in the price of the chassis which had been ordered of £331 each, but another shock was to come: Dennis had taken a cold economic look at the viability of the project and was in the process of deciding to cease production!

Once the general manager became aware of this he suggested that, as a temporary measure, the corporation purchase three second-hand Bristol K5G/ECWs from UCOC, at £250 each. These buses ideally fulfilled the shortage of vehicles, and brought the fleet up to strength pending the supply of other new buses. These were pre-war chassis of 1940 vintage ENOC fleet Nos 3825, 3828 and 3835n and UC Nos 677, 680 and 687. New LCT fleet numbers were allocated, 89, 90 and 91, to replace those same numbers recently withdrawn. This was done simply because these were not new vehicles and seen as temporary to the fleet. These vehicles had been re-fitted with 8ft bodies by ECW in 1953. An interesting publication exists for those interested, explaining the history of these and other vehicles sharing the registration Nos JEV411–435: *The tale of the Wandering JEVs*, by Graham Ledger, published by the Essex Bus Enthusiasts Group.

The LCT vehicles were JEV416, 419 and 426. No.90 (JEV426) carried chassis No.55065 on its p.s.v. licence, which actually belonged to CAP221 of Brighton and Hove district! The certificates

88. Dennis Loline fleet No.163

89. The Ultimate ticket machine had now been in use for some ten years.

90. Fleet No.89 (second issue) Bristol K5G ECW. Former UCOC.

lasted until October 1965. The vehicles were disposed of in January 1966 to a Yorkshire dealer; the engines went to Hong Kong. These vehicles gave sterling service over their four to five years with LCT. For what had been a minimal cost of £250 each, they represented good value. They were used mainly on school and works services.

By the end of September the second Dennis order was cancelled due to what Dennis described as 'a temporary cessation of PSV vehicle chassis manufacture.' They informed the corporation that in the circumstances they would accept total cancellation of the order. Bearing in mind the uncertainty of the Dennis order, the general manager reported on the possibility of purchasing another style of low-bridge chassis then being developed by Leyland Ltd. Demands had been made by various municipalities that Leyland produce a new low-height vehicle with a Leyland engine. As a result, Leyland decided to develop the Lowlander, which would be produced by Albion Motors, a subsidiary based in Glasgow. No doubt based on the well-founded success of previous Leyland products, many orders were forthcoming from municipalities, which justified the project. The general manager had informed East Lancs. Coachbuilders, with whom the council had a contract to supply bodies supposedly for the Dennis vehicles, of a possible delay in the supply of suitable chassis, and was satisfied that the company would accept the delay provided they were assured of receiving suitable chassis in due course. The council authorised the cancellation of the Dennis contract. The general manager investigated further the suitability of the Leyland chassis under development, and, as a result of this, East Lancs. Coachbuilders. were advised that they would ultimately be provided with chassis in accordance with the existing contract.

On 1 October 1961 major service changes were introduced within the Luton district transport coordinated area:

In November 1961 the general manager drew the council's attention to the capital expenditure programme for replacement buses. He reported that there was a need for twelve buses for 1962/63, which included a provision for four additional buses. The considered view was that a further twenty-one buses were needed during the three years from 1963 to 1966, plus a further four as a provision. The new Leyland low-bridge chassis would be called the Albion Lowlander, and the price for each chassis would be £3,008.18. This was cheaper than the Dennis. Six were ordered, and notice was given to East Lancs. Coachbuilders of the available chassis. In December 1962 an order for a further ten Albion Lowlanders was placed with Leyland, and loans for sixteen applied for.

91. Dennis Loline 11 East Lancs. Fleet No. 164.

In January 1962 quotations were received from East Lancs. Coachbuilders for sixty-five-seat bodies with sliding doors, at £3,299.16 each. An alternative, with jack-knife doors, would be £3,328.6 each. These vehicles were 10in longer than the Dennis Loline, allowing room for two more seats. The sliding door type was ordered.

Meanwhile, plans forged ahead with the new depot. A negotiated tender price was agreed with H.C. Janes Ltd, a large local builder, for the construction of the new depot costing £110,425.0.8d. A loan was sought from the Ministry of Transport for £47,051. The balance was available from the disposal of assets to be replaced after deducting outstanding debt.

Six quotations were received for ten Albion Lowlanders, including sixty-five and seventy-seat options at 28ft 6in and 30ft lengths respectively. East Lancs. Coachbuilders, the second lowest, was accepted. An order was placed for sixty-five-seat bodies, at a total cost of £32,930.

The Transport Coordination Joint Committee had continued to meet monthly since the 1948 agreement commenced. A wage increase of 6s 6d per week was approved nationally, with effect from 20 May 1962. Consequently this resulted in additional costs of £9,000 P/A, and a fare revision was sought and agreed for implementation on 12 August. In February the bonus deviation payment was agreed to be continued at 7s per week, provided duties of forty-eight hours per week were completed. The union had sought an increase, in view of inflation, to 11s. In September 1962 it was resolved that all new crew employed by LCT would not be entitled to benefit from the conditions of service negotiated locally, i.e. bonus deviation payments for a forty-eight-hour week, unless they belonged to the appropriate trade union.

The general manager reported on the practicality of fitting fluorescent lights in the ten new Albion Lowlanders on order. East Lancs. Coachbuilders quoted an extra £128 per bus, which was agreed upon and the order amended. It was also agreed that, following the move to the new depot, the general manager would become responsible for repair and maintenance of all corporation vehicles, including the fleet of dustcarts. In view of this, it was necessary to transfer engineering staff from the borough engineering department to the transport department.

At the end of January 1963 crew numbers remained stable at 239, against a full complement requirement of 244. On 29 April the new Kingsway depot became fully operational, the transfer having been gradually accomplished over the previous month. This fully replaced the former depot in Park Street, Luton, which you will recall had been extended from the former tram depot. Nationally unions were pressing for a forty-hour week, which was rejected.

In view of the combined council vehicle maintenance requirements the corporation considered the future policy of vehicle and plant purchases. So far as it was practical, it was resolved that a standard colour scheme be adopted, and that there should be a standardisation of all vehicles.

The Beeching Report on the railways was very topical in April 1963. The council was concerned at the possible effects of his recommendations. Railway stations at Bute Street, Luton, Hoo, Dunstable North and Dunstable town were to be closed. There would no longer be a rail link between Dunstable, Luton and Hatfield. The council agreed to consider what, if any, alternative transport was required.

With effect from 18 April 1963 a national pay increase was awarded of 8s 9d per week. This would cost the corporation £12,000 P/A. An increase was also under consideration for the engineers and craftsmen. Again, a fare increase was sought. Following the pay increase, the FMPTE contacted the corporation regarding the bonus deviation payments and stated that, in view of the national increase, the undertaking would rescind or reduce the deviation payment scheme. LCT replied that it did not wish to either rescind or reduce it, no doubt realising that such a change would spark off local labour relation difficulties.

In May the drivers requested the installation of cab heaters in those buses not already fitted with them. The corporation agreed that heaters should be fitted to thirty-four buses which were likely to remain in service for a reasonable period. The total cost of the installation was £1,020. Despite earlier consideration having been given to adopting a standard colour scheme, in June 1963 the borough council confirmed that the buses should remain in the existing red livery. Airport fire tenders would be orange, police cars and ambulances black and cream respectively, and all other vehicles dark green.

A revision of service timetables was undertaken in late 1963. On 30 September representatives of Lincoln Corporation Transport were entertained to lunch. The visit was arranged to discuss their

92. Albion Lowlander fleet No.174 showing original stairs window which was panelled in by LCT as shown in the picture of 175.

93. Albion Lowlander fleet No.175.

94. Albion Lowlander LR7 fleet No.173.

idea of a possible coordination of their undertaking with that of another operator in the area. Clearly the discussions came to nothing. The sixteen Albion LR7 with East Lancs. bodies were delivered throughout 1963.

The Southern Counties Touring Society visited the depot on Sunday 6 October 1963, and were provided free transport in one of the new Albions with sliding doors and air suspension. As was customary they were also entertained to tea, this time at the airport restaurant. By November 1963 the crew situation was deteriorating again, now standing at 233 against a requirement of 252. A one-day strike of all crew occurred on Friday 20 December. The reason is not known, but there was a return to work the following day with a meeting scheduled for 6 January 1964. Nothing further is recorded.

On 26 January 1964 various changes to the LCT and UC-operated route numbers and routes within the Luton District Transport agreement were implemented. These can be traced in Appendix 8 (Route Information).

By January 1964 three Crossley double-deck buses were surplus to requirements. One was adapted as a replacement to the existing mobile staff canteen. The remaining two were de-licensed and used as spare parts for the remaining Crossleys in the fleet.

Another national pay award was granted on 13 February with increases of 14s p/w for drivers and 10s 6d p/w for conductors. It was reckoned that this was creating a burden of another £13,600 P/A on wage costs. A fare revision was sought and approved, with effect from 31 March 1964. There is a glimpse of the retirement conditions for conductors recorded for a Mr F.W. Brown, aged sixty-one, who retired on 1 April 1964, after forty years' service. He was awarded a lump sum of £356.14.5d and an annual pension of the same amount.

Later deliveries of the Albion Lowlanders had Neepsend bodies, again with sliding doors. All of these vehicles proved troublesome, LCT having specified variations during initial construction. The vehicles were heavy, the suspension did not stand up to the task, the air systems which operated the rear suspension and the doors constantly failed through leakage. Gearboxes and transmissions proved unreliable. The troublesome air suspension at the rear was gradually replaced by coil springs, commencing in 1969. A triangular glass window on the lower landing of the staircase was in the original specification but was removed during 1967. It is interesting to note that since delivery of the Leyland PD2s in 1948, despite various chassis and bodies, all vehicles in the fleet had Leyland 9.8-litre o–600 oil engines, with varying brake horse power ratings.

C1 LCT fleet No.104 low–bridge, delivered in 1948.

C2 Leyland PD2/1 121 waiting in Wellington Street, the Luton town terminus for route 6 (note the coloured radiator surround). This picture clearly illustrates the practice of painted advertisements of the time.

C3 Fleet No.132 Leyland PD2/10 Farington, delivered in 1954, pictured later in its life, in a pillar box red with cream band above the lower deck.

C4 Fleet No.149 seen at Park Square with an all-over pillar box red livery.

C5 Leyland PD2/22 MCW fleet No.157 at a temporary bus station outside the library.

C6 Dennis Loline 11 East Lancs. fleet No.164.

C7 Leyland Albion Lowlander LR7 No.170.

C8 Leyland Albion LR7 East Lancs. fleet No.174, delivered in 1963.

C9 Leyland PD2/2, thought to be fleet No.115, later in its life as it stands in the Kingsway depot.

C10 Leyland line–up at Kingsway depot.

C11 Leyland Albion LR7 Neepsend fleet No.175 pictured at a developing Luton Airport.

C12 Dennis Loline No.181.

C13 Dennis Loline III Neepsend fleet No.184 'Looking rather scruffy'.

C14 Dennis Loline III Neepsend fleet No.183 Dennis Loline and Bristol Lodeka. Two of a kind!

C15 Pre-delivery shot of a LCT RELL at ECW works, Lowestoft.

C16 Bristol RELL6L ECW fleet No.109 en route to Luton Airport.

C17 Fleet No.130 Bristol RELL6L ECW semi-auto, pictured after takeover by UC, still operating in it's LCT livery.

C18 A rather mixed group at Kingsway Garage, following takeover. Note the Albion in UC livery.

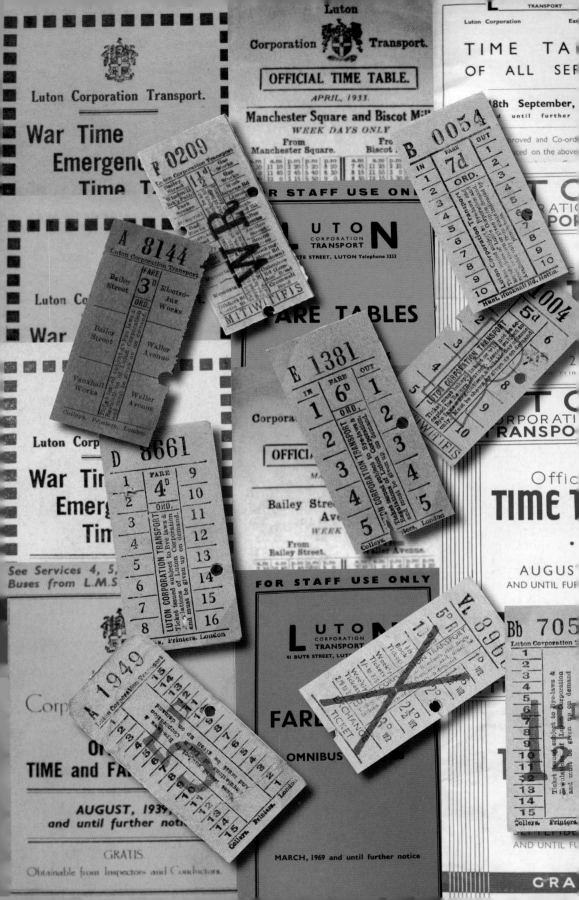

95. Leyland Albion LR7 Neepsend fleet No.179, pictured on a football special for Luton Town Football Club.

96. Leyland Albion LR7 Neepsend fleet No.170 showing nearside view and sliding door.

Since early 1963 the population of Luton had risen to 155,000. LCT fleet completed some 2,741,000 miles in that year. In April 1964 something like a minor political revolution was taking place at the borough council. A councillor had proposed:

> that the council had no confidence in the ability of the majority group as represented by the Labour party members of the council to formulate and implement a policy that would ensure the efficient and financially self supporting operation of the Corporation Passenger Transport undertaking and that the General Purposes Committee be instructed to take prompt and positive action.

Clearly things were not good, as we shall see later. In fact, the financial position was getting progressively worse.

A scheduled order for ten further double-deck buses was reduced to six to replace the nine remaining Crossleys. Quotations were sought from both Leyland and Dennis (who had re-commenced chassis building). The order was placed with Dennis for six Loline Mk IIIs fitted with the familiar Leyland 0600 engines at a cost of £3,208 each. A typical week's revenue at this time was around £10,000. Crews were still below the full complement at 235 against a requirement of 252. A further fare revision was sought and implemented in late May. Six quotations were received for the supply and fitting of bodies to the six Dennis chassis. The East Lancs. quote was accepted at £21,720.

In July 1964 a report was presented on the current arrangements for the coordination agreement and a possible extension of the arrangements. A significant development in 1964 was the opening of the central bus station on Sunday 9 August. Hitherto buses had terminated at various points in the town. It was, however, only a temporary affair, and only partially fulfilled the need. The bus station was located at the corner of Williamson Street and Guilford Street, only to be replaced in 1969 by yet another temporary but larger bus station in an area of demolition between Bridge Street and Williamson Street, in front of the then new central library. Guilford Street and Williamson Street have since disappeared, swallowed up in the development of the Arndale centre.

The salary of General Manager Mr Wickens was, at this time, £3,180 P/A. In November wages and conditions were again on the agenda. The Transport and General Workers Union (TGWU) proposed a merit bonus scheme which was rejected by LCT. Conductors applied for the existing deviation bonus to be increased to 30s, and in support of this proposed an overtime and rest day ban with effect from 25 November 1964. LCT responded that they would only consider the increase if the threat of a ban were lifted. Whilst these local wrangles continued, a substantial national pay claim had been lodged. The borough council consulted the FMPTE to ascertain their views, because although the TGWU had withdrawn its application for a merit scheme, conductors had adopted a 'work to rule', with effect from 1 December 1964, and submitted a revised claim for the deviation payment to be increased from 11s to 21s p/w.

In early January 1965 the Ministry of Transport approved the closure of the Hatfield–Luton–Dunstable railway line, subject to suitable alternative transport being available. By mid-January 1965 the national pay claim had been referred to arbitration, and an award of 15s for crew and 13s 6d for depot staff had been approved. This would add a further £17,000 to the wage bill, prompting another request for a fare revision, which was approved and implemented on 23 May 1965. In August 1965 Mr C.S.A. Wickens was approaching his sixty-fifth birthday. The borough council extended his employment until 31 January 1966 in order to be given time to arrange for a suitable replacement. He had been with LCT since 5 August 1939, over twenty-six years, and on 29 March 1965 completed fifty years service in the bus industry, having joined London General as a boy of fifteen. Public advertisements for the post of general manager at a starting salary of £3,260 were placed in the PSV press.

By March 1965 crew numbers were down again at 234, against a full complement 256, LCT continued to advertise. At the end of May 1965 the NJIC permitted an increase in the bonus deviation payment to 16s. LCT had meanwhile gone ahead and paid an increase to 20s without the approval of NJIC. As a result LCT was advised that they were no longer considered as being in membership and not permitted to attend the AGM. In an unusual move LCT sought the support of the TGWU in an effort to continue the payment at 20s.

The national spiral of wage increases and inflation was again evident when East Lancs. advised LCT that the six bus bodies on order would cost an extra £432 each due to wage increases.

In September 1965 eight applications for the post of general manager were considered. Applications had been received from personnel already working for the following undertakings: Stockton-on-Tees, Manchester (2), West Bromwich, Caerphilly, Reading, Bradford and Luton. The post was offered to Mr Rufas Max Carl Baschy, the existing deputy general manager of Stockton-on-Tees Corporation Transport who would commence with LCT on 1 February 1966.

The local TGWU made a further application for an increase in October 1965. As LCT was no longer part of FMPTE they were not party to decisions made by NJIC and realised that they would need to establish local negotiating machinery.

In late 1965 the last six double-deckers to be purchased arrived. These were the Dennis Loline 111s. Certain Gardner parts were fitted into Leyland engines to enable them to fit the chassis. Eight older buses were de-licensed and withdrawn; these were the three ex-UCOC Bristols and five of the Crossleys. These were sold to Dennis Higgs & Son of Monks Bretton, near Barnsley. Weekly revenues had improved at between £10–12,000. Crew numbers were also looking better at 254 against a full requirement of 256.

A special meeting was held on 15 December 1965 between the town clerk, the borough treasurer and the transport general manager, with a view to report on all aspects of the transport undertaking in which it might be possible to effect improvements in the economic operation of services. The following is a report of that meeting:

1. Revision of frequencies of services with a view to eliminating, where possible, uneconomic operation during both peak and off-peak times.
2. To submit a report on the possibility of re-organising existing services on a more economic basis.
3. To adjust the principle that no substantial change should be made in the standard off peak services and that in off-peak hours a reasonable public service should be maintained.
4. That the general manager in consultation with borough treasurer report at an early meeting on possibility of introducing one man operated buses to the maximum extent with particular reference to the following:

   a) Phasing of introduction of such vehicles
   b) Expenditure involved
   c) Method of fare collection
   d) Anticipated savings in operating costs

As an outcome of the special meeting, in February 1966 the new general manager, Mr Baschy, was instructed to investigate the practicality of purchasing up to ten single-deck vehicles suitable for one-man operation and report in detail! He was also tasked with providing a full report on all aspects of the undertaking to be available by June 1966. Another revision of fares was under consideration. The possibility of flashing indicators being fitted to all those buses not so fitted was considered at this time, but no decision was made.

In February 1966 LCT was re-admitted membership of the FMTPE, and a formal application was made to ratify the current wages, terms and conditions of employees. The general manager reported that the NJIC intended to submit a proposal for a substantial increase in wages. At the end of March 1966 eight buses were withdrawn: seven Crossleys and one Daimler.

The general manager reported on the possibility of one-man-operated buses, and recommended the purchase of ten single-deck buses for delivery during 1966/67. It was agreed that quotations should be obtained for chassis and bodies. On 27 May 1966 the general manager submitted his report on all aspects of the undertaking.

Plans were announced to replace all rear-entrance double-deck buses with one-man-operated vehicles and conversion of the twenty-four front entrance Lolines and Lowlanders to one man operation was begun. These steps were taken in order to reduce the ever-increasing deficit. In August 1966 quotations were accepted from Bristol Commercial Vehicles Ltd (BCV) for five Bristol RELL 6L chassis, at £2,937.10 each. These buses had a four-speed synchromesh gearbox. ECW would provide one-man-operation bodies with forty-eight-seat dual three-step entrances. Six of the Leyland PD2s and the

97. Dennis Loline III Neepsend fleet No.183 at Luton's temporary bus station.

remainder of the Crossley spares were disposed of. An earlier application for a fare increase was deferred for six months as a result of a Ministry of Transport directive for a nationwide standstill on fares.

In November 1966 the advertising agents W.H. Smith & Son Ltd drew attention to the reduced size of the fleet from eighty-one at the time of their agreement with LCT to the current figure of sixty-eight. They argued that the guaranteed minimum payment of £4,121 be reduced proportionally to £3,460.

Bristol Commercial Vehicles (BCV) approached the corporation and recommended the installation of an air-assisted clutch mechanism costing £21 per chassis. This was agreed to. Meanwhile, Leyland Motors agreed to place at LCT's disposal a Leyland Panther Cub single-deck one-man-operated bus for the week commencing 7 November 1966. Following this quotations were sought for a further five single-deck chassis. Fifteen quotes were received, and BCV Bristol RELLs were accepted, with the same specification as before, at a cost of £2,974.8 each.

On 21 December 1966 the local TGWU reacted to the idea of one-man-operated buses and laid down the following terms:

- Rest day working discontinued, all overtime to be before or after normal duties.
- Platform staff not prepared to co-operate in use of one man operated vehicles until certain matters had been agreed to their satisfaction.
- No trainees would be accepted.
- Hours worked by conductors should be in accord with those prescribed in the Road Traffic Act for drivers of p.s.v.s

In February 1967 it was announced that smoking would be prohibited in the front half of the new single-deck buses. Twenty-five Almex ticket-issuing machines for one-man-operated buses were purchased, costing £2,000. Flashing indicators were fitted on twenty of the older double-deck buses, at a cost of £50 each. Six further Leyland PD2s were disposed of to Hartwood Finance Ltd.

Quotes were sought and accepted from ECW for five single-deck bodies, costing £3,516.5 each. Delivery of the first five single-deck vehicles came in June 1967. They were licensed for eighteen standing passengers but had no other room than the standard gangway. The idea was that these would enter service on 2 July 1967.

LCT purchased a further seventy-five Almex ticket machines at a cost of £6,000. In June 1967 the Transport Committee resolved that all future vehicle replacements would be single-deckers suitable for one-man-operation of the type currently under contract. A further ten units were then ordered from BCV and ECW, for delivery in spring 1968. These and all those subsequently ordered would have four-speed semi-automatic gearboxes.

Delivery of the first batch was not without difficulty. The crews were most unhappy at the prospect of redundancies and extra responsibilities. A number of vehicles were stranded in the Kingsway depot for some while after being sabotaged with sawdust in the fuel, and they eventually entered service on the airport circular routes 29, 31 and 32, following the withdrawal of the remaining Crossleys and Leyland PD2/1s of 1948. The RELLs were the first Bristols of their type to enter service with a municipal operator in the UK. The buses operated on routes 6, 29, 30, 31, 32, 45 and 54 during their first year. The delayed fare revision was introduced on 2 July 1967.

Services 29, 30 and 31 were varied to provide a direct connection between the LMR Station and the airport. Discussions with advertising agents W.H. Smith & Son took place concerning advertising on the single-deck buses. In July a committee was established by the Ministry of Transport to study passenger transport coordination with a view to securing a more effective and co-ordinated service in the southeast region.

Quotations were received in late August 1967 for ten Bristol Chassis with Leyland 600 engines and semi-automatic gearboxes, at £3,209.17.3d each, with coachwork by ECW at £3,515.15 each. Quotations were sought for ten more buses for delivery in 1968/69. Disposal of nine Leyland PD2s took place. No. 116 was retained for driver instruction purposes. Staff levels in mid-October 1967 were 119 drivers and ninety-nine conductors, against a requirement of 126 and ninety-five respectively.

There were more labour problems in late October 1967. The council were informed of the breakdown at a national level of negotiations concerning revisions of the national agreement. The trade union side of the NJIC had terminated the national agreement regulating wages and conditions with effect from 12 October 1967, and withdrew from the NJIC. It was their expressed intention to endeavour to negotiate agreements, failing which certain embargoes would be imposed. The local TGWU sought an early meeting with LCT which was agreed and conveyed on 23 October. Notwithstanding this, the following embargoes were brought into effect at midnight on 25 October 1967.

- A total ban on standing passengers.
- A total ban on voluntary overtime from 6 November 1967, meaning that no employee worked more than forty hours per week. This incidentally forfeited their right to a deviation payment of £1 per week and meant that they were in breach of the forty-six-hour minimum agreement.
- Non co-operation in the further implementation or extension of one-man operation.

98. Dennis Loline III Neepsend fleet No.182 at Luton town centre temporary bus station.

99. Bristol RELL fleet No. 105.

Representatives of the TGWU met with LCT and requested that local negotiating machinery be set up and referred to a claim for a local agreement for:

- Higher minimum wage.
- Shorter working hours and other modifications of the former national agreement.

LCT declined to set up local negotiating machinery, following which a sub-committee was set up to consider the situation generally. Meanwhile, the council sub-committee authorised LCT to take any action necessary to maintain services having regard to the labour resources available. Any eventual agreement reached would, in any event, be subject to the scrutiny of the prices and incomes policy and be reported to the Ministry of Transport.

The effect of the embargoes was such that in many instances drivers were left without conductors, and visa-versa. In order to maintain services it was necessary to pair unattached drivers and conductors to make up a crew. This inevitably meant that either one or the other had to relinquish their scheduled duty to take up the other, and in many cases had to accept a meal break at a different time to that allocated.

One incident occurred where a driver and two conductresses had been suspended from duty, on 29 November 1967, for failing to carry out their respective duties in accordance with instructions issued to them on behalf of LCT management. This resulted in an approach from the TGWU on 30 November with a notice to withdraw total labour unless LCT rescinded the suspension and restored lost wages. They considered that the event was caused by the 'management's wilful and wrongful breach of present and past customs, practice and agreement on duty schedules'.

LCT was in a corner: they offered re-instatement to the three employees, from 30 November. The three failed to return to work! The TGWU had brought the withdrawal of labour into effect from midnight on 30 November 1967. The buses did not operate for just over two weeks, and employees returned to work on 19 December 1967. Following crisis talks, LCT upheld management action in suspending the three employees who were then re-instated and, as a gesture, offered re-imbursements for lost pay for the period of suspension, subject to LCT's future ability to amend schedules and meal breaks. The union prevaricated on minor points but held that they would want two days notice of meal break changes! Crews returned to work on 19 December 1967. Services were maintained as best as possible.

100. Fleet No.105 Bristol RELL6L ECW pictured outside Luton LMR station showing the dual doors for entry and exit.

In early December 1967 LCT had received quotes for a further ten single-deck buses with the same specification, at £3,209.17.3*d* each for the chassis and engines. A test was at that time being carried out on one vehicle of a hydraulic fuel pump, and it was advised that these could be fitted at an extra cost of £60 per vehicle.

On 14 December 1967 the FMPTE and the employees trade unions agreed an increase of £1 per week and a forty-hour week, with effect from the next full pay period.

On 11 January 1968 the NJIC ratified the proposed pay and conditions agreement, but on 26 January 1968 the Prices and Incomes Board prohibited the implementation for three months from 27 January 1968, or until the board reported on the matter further. Six members of LCT staff had instituted proceedings in the County Court against LCT, claiming payment of the additional £1 per week as ratified by the NJIC. The solicitor for the council entered a defence referring to the relevant provisions of the Prices and Incomes Act, which prevented LCT from implementing the agreement.

On 30 January 1968 compulsory purchase orders of 53 Waller Street and 37 and 39 Williamson Street took place to make way for further land for the next temporary bus station. By mid-February 1968 staff numbers were dropping, drivers numbered 102 and conductors 100 against a requirement of 126 and ninety-five respectively. Particular difficulties were being experienced with the shortage of drivers. Ten more single-deck buses had commenced delivery, Nos 111–120, but were not immediately put into service due to a shortage of drivers. Further obsolete Leyland double-deck buses were disposed of. The general manager was asked to undertake a review of routes and frequencies, and submit a report to contain cost, in addition to the extension of one-man operations, to achieve a more economic overall operation.

ECW submitted a quote in late March 1968 for ten new bodies, to be Nos 121–130, at £3,653 each. At the end of April the general manager sought permission from the council to employ part-time seasonal labour, as recommended by the Prices and Incomes Board, to alleviate difficulties experienced in operating services. Approval was given and the TGWU consulted.

In June 1968 the TGWU sought written assurance that at the end of the period of standstill, payment of the £1 per week would be made with effect from 14 December 1967. Difficulties still existed with the transfer of crews to one-man operation. The Prices and Income Board had made a recommendation on 15 December 1967 that an acceptance allowance of 10*s* per week should be paid to all staff where there was a firm agreement for the introduction and extension of one-man operations. The report also included recommendations in respect of increased premium rates for the drivers of certain one-man-operated buses, with locally negotiated agreements in certain circumstances. On 13 June 1968 the NJIC approved a national agreement along the lines recommended by the Prices and Incomes Board affecting undertakings that ran one-man-operated buses. They also recommended that the matter of the £1 increase from 14 December 1967 be referred to the Secretary of State for Employment for consideration.

At the council meeting held on 9 July the borough treasurer reported on the financial position of the bus undertaking with some concern. The accumulated deficiency on 31 March 1968 was £154,786, with provisions for a further deficiency of £23,765 for the current financial year. He was also concerned that anticipated savings in running costs were not being seen due to the delay in bringing into service ten recently delivered single-deck buses. This had arisen as a result of the reluctance of the staff to agree to the extension of one-man operations at that time. Further extra expenditure would arise as a result of a bonus payment to workshop staff approved by the Ministry of Housing and local government. There was also the question of the unknown additional liability of increased wages, still the subject of protracted negotiations at national level, and of outstanding issues with the Secretary of State for Employment and Productivity.

In July 1968 the general manager reported on a review of routes and frequencies, and submitted recommendations which if adopted would affect an operating economy of £20,000 in a full year. A revision of routes and frequencies was proposed and adopted, and can be traced in Appendix 8 (Route Information).

Preliminary negotiations took place in 1968 with UC regarding the future of the coordination agreement, which was due to expire in January 1970. The general managers of both LCT and UC prepared and submitted a fares revision for the co-ordinated area, to produce an increase in the pool revenue of £40,000 P/A. The pay issue, meanwhile, dragged on. A local agreement was offered to the local TGWU, based upon the agreement made by the FMPTE, in December 1967 (in terms acceptable to the government), but, of course, LCT could not clarify that the £1 offered would be backdated as this was still in the hands of the Secretary of State. As anticipated, the TGWU rejected the offer on 11 August 1968 and stated that until a written assurance was given the originally proposed increase of £1 per week would be paid retrospectively from December 1967, and there would be no further extension of one-man operations.

The local agreement offered incorporated a general increase of 10s per week from 14 December 1967, and a further acceptance bonus of 10s per week from June 1968, conditional upon staff co-operating in existing and future extensions of one-man operations. It did, however, require a withdrawal of the £1 per week, from December 1967, but did provide for an increase in premium rates for one-man operations to 20 per cent for single-deck and 22.5 per cent for double-deck buses.

The union sought further negotiations and submitted a draft claim for the payment of the £1 per week retrospectively from December 1967, plus the 10s acceptance bonus as offered, the 20 per cent premium rate for single-deck drivers with a greater per cent to be negotiated for double-deck drivers. Clearly LCT saw no purpose in such a meeting as they were unable to offer the £1 retrospectively, remaining in contravention of the government prices and incomes policy.

The general manager of UC wrote to LCT stating that consideration had been given to certain inherent disadvantages arising from the operation of two transport undertakings in Luton, and that the conclusion had been reached that many of these would disappear under single ownership. They enquired whether the council would consider an examination-taking place with a view to the possible acquisition of the Corporation Transport undertaking by UC. Understandably the council approved an examination on the basis that this would not commit the council to the disposal of the undertaking, but they must have been rubbing their hands gleefully!

In mid-October 1968 a meeting was convened between the local TGWU and LC. The union stood its ground. LCT agreed that it would pay the £1 retrospectively, as sought, provided that it was not prevented from doing so by government legislation or the NJIC. This offer was conditional upon the TGWU accepting the provisions of the NJIC agreement of November 1965, including clauses relating to the introduction of one-man-operated services, and that the 10s acceptance bonus should be deemed as included in the rates of pay set out in the agreement of December 1967. Needless to say, the TGWU rejected this offer at their meeting on 20 October 1968, stating that the TGWU expected LC, on 26 December 1968, the date on which the standstill imposed by the government would expire, to fully honour the agreement of 14 December 1967 by making the retrospective payments.

101. Bristol RELL6L ECW fleet No.114.

The recent revision of fares application was approved and commenced on 27 October 1968. Staffing at LCT remained a problem, not only with regard to the ongoing pay and conditions difficulties, but numbers were down to levels which made it difficult to operate satisfactorily, bearing in mind the embargoes implemented by the unions. In early October 1968 driver levels were 101 and conductors eighty-five, against a requirement of 126 and ninety-five respectively. On 29 November 1968 a public hearing was held concerning proposed modifications to services 42, 43, 50, 51 and 52. By 13 November 1968 staff numbers had again dropped to ninety-eight drivers and eighty-four conductors. LCT asked the Department of Employment to receive a deputation from the council to discuss the staffing and pay difficulties. This took place on 18 November 1968, but served only to permit the council to outline the problems. Following this meeting LCT pressed the FMPTE to make known to the government the need for implementation of the pay award of 14 December 1967.

On 19 December 1968 the TGWU accepted the council's proposals for implementation of the pay provisions of the agreement of 14 December 1967, subject to clarifying a counter-proposal relating to the premium rate payable to one man operated drivers. This matter was left in abeyance until a decision on premium rates was reached at a national level. Records are unfortunately unclear as to what the final agreement was. We presume that it was the most recent offer by LCT, in mid-October 1968. Whether the 10s acceptance bonus was paid in addition or within this sum remains unclear. Whatever the deal, at last the embargoes could be lifted, but it would be too late to save the undertaking.

By the end of 1968 some thirty new single-deckers had been purchased, although eighteen had remained in store as a result of the embargoes. During 1969 the corporation were able to introduce further one-man operation and it is believed they brought fourteen single-deckers, previously held in store, into operation. Nos 127–130 remained in store. A fare revision application was submitted to the Traffic Commissioner .

In January 1969 staff numbers had reduced even further to ninety-seven drivers, and eighty-one conductors, against a requirement of 126 and ninety-five respectively. Following the pay and conditions agreement, with the embargoes lifted, service 6 was converted to a one man operation on 16 February 1969.

An order for five thirty-seven-seat one-man-operated small Bristol LH 56P single-deck buses was placed with ECW. These had Perkins 6354 oil engines. The chassis quotation from Bristol was £2,035 each, while the bodies were quoted at £2,673 each. These were the first vehicles ordered since 1948 without a Leyland engine. They were intended for eventual use on the Cutenhoe Road–Fountains

102. Meant to have been fleet No.134, this Bristol LHS6P ECW stands at the depot.

Road services, in a revised form where turning capacities were limited. The vehicles were delivered in November 1969 but never entered service with LCT. An order was placed early in 1969 for five Bristol RELL6Gs, but with Gardner engines rather than Leyland. Chassis costs were £3,831.13 each, and bodies by ECW cost £3,910 each. These would have become fleet Nos 136–145, to be delivered to UC in February 1970. One has to ask the question whether the departure at this stage from Leyland engines was due to any influence by UC who, of course, were familiar with Gardner.

In April 1969 LCT had to pay UC £3,527. This was due to reduced mileages induced by shortage of staff and the embargoes between April 1968 and February 1969.

Modifications were approved for the five Bristol LHs to be fitted with an auxiliary air reservoir at a cost of £75 each. The ten RELL6Gs were fitted with a battery isolation switch, a wet tank and an automatic drain valve to the air braking system, at £221 each.

By late May 1969 staffing had improved little. Drivers numbered 105 and conductors sixty-four, against a requirement of 124 and seventy-three respectively. LCT purchased a reconditioned Bedford RL 4x4 breakdown truck. In August 1969 discussions took place with the TGWU on the conversion of service 45 to a one-man operation. At the end of October 1969 the council received an offer for the transport undertaking from UC. Audited accounts for the year ending March 1969 showed a deficit of £226,000.

At the council meeting on 3 November 1969 sale of the Corporation Transport undertaking was agreed subject to ministerial consent, as contained in the offer letter from UC dated 27 October 1969. Acceptance of the offer was formally communicated to UC on 11 November 1969. Basically the terms of the final sale agreement are summarised as follows:

- UC to pay Luton Borough Council £294,824, which included £45,000 goodwill in respect of the following assets: seventy-seven public service vehicles, two cars, one van, and 100 Amex ticket machines.
- Purchase at cost price of all unused uniforms and unused mechanical spares.
- UC to offer employment on the council's existing terms and conditions to all persons employed by the transport undertaking.

- UC to accept the council's liabilities for present and future superannuation benefits.
- UC to accept assignment of all contracts, agreements or other obligations entered into by the council for the purpose of the transport undertaking.
- UC to pay the appropriate portion of the fees payable on all p.s.v. licences.
- UC to have use of part of the Kingsway bus depot and transport department offices for a limited period.

Although the date of the takeover was fixed for 1 January 1970, for administrative and legal purposes, particularly for the staff, disposal was changed to Sunday 4 January 1970. At takeover the fleet consisted of forty-seven double-deck buses, including one withdrawn for driver instruction, thirty-five single-deck buses, including nine in store since new, Nos 127–135, and one under repair at a local coachbuilder.

For me, at least, this marks the end of an era.

APPENDIX I

FLEET LIST

Fleet No.	Licence No.	Type	New – Withdrawn
I	TM9876	Daimler CH6 Duple B32R	03/32 – 1944
2	TM9877	Daimler CH6 Duple B32R (da)	03/32 – 08/40
3	TM9880	Daimler CH6 Duple B32R	03/32 – 1940
4	TM9879	Daimler CH6 Duple B32R	03/32 – 1944
5	TM9878	Daimler CH6 Duple B32R	03/32 – 1944
6	TM9882	Daimler CH6 Duple B32R	03932 – 1944
7	TM9881	Daimler CP6 Duple L26/26R (With new Poppet valve petrol engine)	03/32 – 1944
8	TM9883	Daimler CH6 Duple L26/26R	03/32 – 1944
9	TM9884	Daimler CH6 Duple L26/26R	03/32 – 05/45
10	MJ183	Daimler CH6 Duple L26/26R	04/32 – 05/45
11	MJ184	Daimler CH6 Duple L26/26R	04/32 – 05/45
12	MJ185	Daimler CH6 Duple L26/26R	04/32 – 1944
13	MJ434	Daimler CH6 Duple L26/26R	06/32 – 04/48
14	MJ433	Daimler CH6 Duple L26/26R	06/32 – 10/47
15	MJ1031	Daimler CH6 Willowbrook B28R	1932 – 1946
16	MJ1587	Daimler CH6 Willowbrook B28R	03/33 – 04/48
17	MJ1578	Daimler CH6 Willowbrook B28R	03/33 – 1940
18	MJ1589	Daimler CH6 Willowbrook L26/26R	04/33 – 1946
19	MJ1590	Daimler CH6 Willowbrook L26/26R (da)	05/33 – 1940
20	VM6401	Dennis E Davidson B32R	1928 – 1935★
21	TM5909	Dennis EV Strachen B32D	1929 – 1935★
22	MT7868	Dennis E Hickman B32 (da)	1928 – 1935★

Fleet No.	Licence No.	Type	New – Withdrawn
23	TM3739	Dennis E Hickman B32	1928 – 1939
24	RO8252	Dennis E Davidson B32	1927 – 1938★
25	TM5910	Dennis EV Strachen B32D	1929 –1938★
26	TM6084	Dennis EV Strachen B32	1930 – 1939
27	JK210	Dennis E Hickman B31	1928 – 1938★
28	TM9539	Dennis Lance Strachen L50R	1931 – 1946
29	VM6402	Dennis E Davidson B32R	1928 – 1935★
20	MJ6126	Daimler COG5 Willowbrook B32R	02/35 – 09/51
21	MJ5076	Daimler CP6 Willowbrook B32R	09/34 – 1948
22	MJ5077	Daimler CP6 Willowbrook B32R	09/34 – 08/40
24	BTM898	Daimler COG5 40 Willowbrook B39R	01/38 – 09/51
25	BTM897	Daimler COG5 40 Willowbrook B39R	01/38 – 09/51
27	BTM900	Daimler COG5 40 Willowbrook B39R	01/38 – 1952
29	MJ4151	Daimler CH6 W .W/bk. L26/26R (da)	05/34 – 09/40
30	MJ2336	Daimler CH6 Willowbrook L26/26R	07/33 – 04/48
31	MJ2337	Daimler CH6 Willowbrook L26/26R	07/33 – 04/48
32	MJ2747	Daimler CH6 Willowbrook L26/26R	09/33 – 04/48
33	MJ2748	Daimler CH6 Willowbrook L26/26R	09/33 – 04/48
34	MJ2749	Daimler CH6 Willowbrook L26/26R	09/33 – 04/48
35	MJ2879	Daimler CH6 Willowbrook L26/26R	11/33 – 04/48
36	MJ2880	Daimler CH6 Willowbrook L26/26R	11/33 – 04/48
37	MJ4152	Daimler CH6 Willowbrook L26/26R	06/34 – 1946
38	MJ5454	Daimler CP6 Willowbrook L26/26R	12/34 – 04/48
39	MJ5455	Daimler CP6 Willowbrook L26/26R	12/34 – 04/48
40	MJ459	Dennis ES Strachen B32R	1932 – 09/38
41	MJ6492	Daimler COG5 Gdnr L26/26R 5LW Willowbrook	04/35 – 1950
42	MJ6493	Daimler COG5 Gdnr L26/26R 5LW Willowbrook	04/35 –1950
43	MJ6494	Daimler COG5 Gdnr L26/26R 5LW Willowbrook	05/35 –1946

Fleet No.	Licence No.	Type	New – Withdrawn
44	MJ6495	Daimler COG5 Gdnr 5LW Willowbrook L26/26R	05/35 – 1946
45	MJ8924	Daimler COG5 40 Willowbrook B39R	11/35 – 1950
46	MJ9057	Daimler COG5 40 Willowbrook B39R	01/36 – 09/51
47	MJ9682	Daimler COG5 40 Willowbrook B39R	03/36 – 1950
48	MJ9681	Daimler COG5 40 Willowbrook B39R	06/36 – 1950
49	ANM257	Daimler COG5 40 Willowbrook B39R	06/36 – 09/51
50	ANM573	Daimler COG5 Gdnr 5LW Willowbrook L26/26R	06/36 – 1949
51	ANM574	Daimler COG5 Gdnr 5LW Willowbrook L26/26R	06/36 – 1954
52	ANM833	Daimler COG5 Gdnr 5LW Willowbrook L26/26R	08/36 –1950
53	ANM834	Daimler COG5 Gdnr 5LW Willowbrook L26/26R	08/36 – 1954
54	ATM969	Daimler COG5 40 Willowbrook B39R	01/37 – 09/51
55	ATM970	Daimler COG5 40 Willowbrook B39R	01/37 – 09/51
56	ATM971	Daimler COG5 40 Willowbrook B39R	01/37 – 09/51
57	AMJ802	Daimler COG5 Gdnr 5LW Willowbrook L26/26R	03/37 – 1950
58	AMJ801	Daimler COG5 Gdnr 5LW Willowbrook L26/26R	03/37 – 1953
59	AMJ816	Daimler COG5 Gdnr 5LW Willowbrook L26/26R	04/37 – 1950
60	BBM245	Bedford WTB Duple B26F	04/37 – 04/48
61	BNM179	Daimler COG5 Gdnr 5LW Willowbrook L26/26R	07/37 – 06/53
62	BNM180	Daimler COG5 Gdnr 5LW Willowbrook L26/26R	07/37 – 06/53
63	BNM181	Daimler COG5 Gdnr 5LW Willowbrook L26/26R	07/37 – 1952
64	BNM182	Daimler COG5 Gdnr 5LW Willowbrook L26/26R	07/37 – 1953
65	BTM119	Daimler COG5 Gdnr 5LW Willowbrook L26/26R	11/37 – 1950

Fleet No.	Licence No.	Type	New – Withdrawn
66	BTM642	Daimler COG5 Gdnr 5LW Willowbrook L26/26R	01/38 – 1953
67	CNM42	Daimler COG5 Gdnr 5LW Willowbrook. L26/26R	09/38 – 1950
68	CNM43	Daimler COG5 Gdnr 5LW Willowbrook L26/26R	09/38 – 1952
69	CNM44	Daimler COG5 Gdnr 5LW Willowbrook L26/26R	09/38 – 1950
70	CNM45	Daimler COG5 Gdnr 5LW Willowbrook L26/26R	09/38 –1954
71	DNM881	Leyland TD7 Brush L27/28R 8.6 litre	05/42 – 1954
72	DNM882	Leyland TD7 Brush L27/28R 8.6 litre	05/42 – 1954
73	DNM883	Leyland TD7 Brush L27/28R 8.6 litre	05/42 – 1954
74	DNM884	Leyland TD7 Brush L27/28R 8.6 litre	05/42 – 1957
75	DTM30	Bristol K5G Gdnr5LW Duple L27/28R 7 litre	08/42 – 1957
76	DTM476	Guy Arab Gdnr5LW Brush L27/28R 7 litre	1943 – 1953
77	DTM477	Guy Arab Gdnr5LW Brush L27/28R 7 litre	1943 – 1953
78	DTM478	Guy Arab Gdnr5LW Brush L27/28R 7 litre	1943 – 1953
79	DTM479	Guy Arab Gdnr5LW Brush L27/28R 7 litre	1943 – 1953
80	DTM480	Daimler CWG5 Gdnr5LW Brush L27/28R 7 litre	1943 – 1956
81	DTM481	Daimler CWG5 Gdnr5LW Brush L27/28R 7 litre	1943 –1956
82	DTM482	Daimler CWG5 Gdnr5LW Brush L27/28R 7 litre	1943 – 1953
83	DTM483	Daimler CWG5 Gdnr5LW Brush L27/28R 7 litre	1943 –1957
84	DMJ84	Bristol K6A AEC7.7 Park. Royal H30/26R	1944 –1956
85	DMJ85	Bristol K6A AEC7.7 Park. Royal H30/26R	1944 –1956
86	DMJ86	Bristol K6A AEC7.7 Park. Royal H30/26R	1945 – 1956
87	DMJ87	Bristol K6A AEC7.7 Park. Royal H30/26R	1945 – 1956
88	EBM88	Bristol K6A AEC7.7 Weymann H30/26R	1946 – 1960

Fleet No.	Licence No.	Type	New – Withdrawn
89	EBM89	Bristol K6A AEC7.7 Weymann H30/26R	1946 – 1960★
90	EBM90	Bristol K6A AEC7.7 Weymann H30/26R	1946 – 1960★
91	EBM91	Bristol K6A AEC7.7 Weymann H30/26R	1946 – 1960★
89	★ JEV419	Bristol K5G ECW ex.-ENOC.L27/28R	1961 – 1965
90	★ JEV426	Bristol K5G ECW ex.-ENOC.L27/28R	1961 – 1965
91	★ JEV416	Bristol K5G ECW ex.-ENOC.L27/28R	1961 – 1965
92	EBM92	Crossley DD42/3T Turbo H30/26R 8.6 litre	1946 – 1963
93	EBM93	Crossley DD42/3T Turbo H30/26R 8.6 litre	1946 – 1963
94	EBM94	Crossley DD42/3T Turbo H30/26R 8.6 litre	1946 – 1963
95	EBM95	Crossley DD42/3T Turbo H30/26R 8.6 litre	1947 – 1963
96	EBM96	Crossley DD42/3T Turbo H30/26R 8.6 litre	08/47 –1963
97	EBM97	Crossley DD42/3T Turbo H30/26R 8.6 litre	08/47 – 1963
98	EBM98	Crossley DD42/3T Turbo H30/26R 8.6 litre	08/47 – 1963
99	EBM99	Crossley DD42/3T Turbo H30/26R 8.6 litre	08/47 – 1963
100	FNM100	Crossley DD42/5T Turbo L27/26R 8.6 litre	11/48 – 1965
101	FNM101	Crossley DD42/5T Turbo L27/26R 8.6 litre	11/48 – 1965
102	FNM102	Crossley DD42/5T Turbo L27/26R 8.6 litre	11/48 – 1965
103	FNM103	Crossley DD42/5T Turbo L27/26R 8.6 litre	11/48 – 1965
104	FNM104	Crossley DD42/5T Turbo L27/26R 8.6 litre	11/48 – 1966
105	FNM105	Crossley DD42/5T Turbo L27/26R 8.6 litre	11/48 – 1965
106	FNM106	Crossley DD42/5T Turbo L27/26R 8.6 litre	1948 – 1966
107	FNM107	Crossley DD42/5T Turbo L27/26R 8.6 litre	1948 – 1966
108	FNM108	Crossley DD42/5T Turbo L27/26R 8.6 litre	1949 – 1966
109	FNM109	Crossley DD42/5 L27/26R.8.6 litre	11/47 – 1963
110	FNM110	Crossley DD42/5 L27/26R.8.6 litre	11/47 – 1963

Fleet No.	Licence No.	Type	New – Withdrawn
111	FNM111	Crossley DD42/5 L27/26R.8.6 litre	11/47 – 1963
112	FNM112	Leyland PD2/1 L27/26R 9.8 litre	04/48 – 1966
113	FNM113	Leyland PD2/1 L27/26R 9.8 litre	04/48 – 1966
114	FNM114	Leyland PD2/1 L27/26R 9.8 litre	04/48 – 1966
115	FNM115	Leyland PD2/1 L27/26R 9.8 litre	04/48 –1966
116	FNM116	Leyland PD2/1 L27/26R 9.8 litre	05/48 – 1967
117	FNM117	Leyland PD2/1 L27/26R 9.8 litre	05/48 – 1966
118	FNM118	Leyland PD2/1 L27/26R 9.8 litre	05/48 – 1967
119	FNM119	Leyland PD2/1 L27/26R 9.8 litre	05/48 – 1967
120	FNM120	Leyland PD2/1 L27/26R 9.8 litre	05/48 – 1967
121	FNM121	Leyland PD2/1 L27/26R 9.8 litre	05/48 – 1967
122	FNM122	Leyland PD2/1 L27/26R 9.8 litre	05/48 – 1966
123	FNM123	Leyland PD2/1 L27/26R 9.8 litre	05/48 –1966
124	LBM124	Leyland PD2/10 Farington L27/28R 9.8 litre	1953 – 09/67
125	LBM125	Leyland PD2/10 Farington L27/28R.9.8 litre	1953 – 09/67
126	LBM126	Leyland PD2/10 Farington L27/28R 9.8 litre	1953 – 09/67
127	LBM127	Leyland PD2/10 Farington L27/28R 9.8 litre	1953 – 11/67
128	LBM128	Leyland PD2/10 Farington L27/28R 9.8 litre	1953 – 09/67
129	MNM129	Leyland PD2/10 Farington L27/28R 9.8 litre	1953 – 1968
130	MNM130	Leyland PD2/10 Farington L27/28R 9.8 litre	1953 – 1969
131	MNM131	Leyland PD2/10 Farington L27/28R 9.8 litre	1953 – 1968
132	MNM132	Leyland PD2/10 Farington L27/28R 9.8 litre	1953 – 1969
133	MNM133	Leyland PD2/10 Farington L27/28R 9.8 litre	1953 – 1969
134	MNM134	Leyland PD2/10 Farington L27/28R 9.8 litre	1954 –1969

Fleet No.	Licence No.	Type	New – Withdrawn
135	MNM135	Leyland PD2/10 Farington L27/28R 9.8 litre	1954 –1969
136	MNM136	Leyland PD2/10 Farington L27/28R 9.8 litre	1954 –12/68
137	MNM137	Leyland PD2/10 Farington L27/28R 9.8 litre	1954 – 1969
138	MNM138	Leyland PD2/10 Farington L27/28R 9.8 litre	1954 – 1968
139	RNM139	Leyland PD2/22 MCW L27/28R	09/56 – 1969 UC
140	RNM140	Leyland PD2/22 MCW L27/28R	1956 – 1970 UC
141	RNM141	Leyland PD2/22 MCW L27/28R	1956 – 1969 UC
142	RNM142	Leyland PD2/22 MCW L27/28R	1956 – 1969 UC
143	RNM143	Leyland PD2/22 MCW L27/28R	1956 –1970 UC
144	RMJ144	Leyland PD2/22 MCW L27/28R	1956 – 1970 UC
145	RMJ145	Leyland PD2/22 MCW L27/28R	1956 – 1970 UC
146	RMJ146	Leyland PD2/22 MCW L27/28R	1956 –1970 UC
147	RMJ147	Leyland PD2/22 MCW L27/28R	1956 – 1970 UC
148	UMN148	Leyland PD2/31 MCW L27/28R	1957 – 1970 UC
149	UNM149	Leyland PD2/31 MCW L27/28R	1957 – 1970 UC
150	UNM150	Leyland PD2/31 MCW L27/28R	1957 – 1970 UC
151	UNM151	Leyland PD2/31 MCW L27/28R	1957 – 1970 UC
152	UNM152	Leyland PD2/31 MCW L27/28R	1957 –1970 UC
153	WTM153	Leyland PD2/30 MCW L27/28R	1959 –1970 UC
154	WTM154	Leyland PD2/30 MCW L27/28R	1959 – 1970 UC
155	WTM155	Leyland PD2/30 MCW L27/28R	1959 – 1970 UC
156	WTM156	Leyland PD2/30 MCW L27/28R	1959 –1970 UC
157	WTM157	Leyland PD2/30 MCW L27/28R	1959 – 1970 UC
158	ANM158	Leyland PD2/30 East Lancs. L27/28R	1960 – 1970 UC
159	ANM159	Leyland PD2/30 East Lancs. L27/28R	1960 – 1970 UC
160	ANM160	Leyland PD2/30 East Lancs. L27/28R	1960 – 1970 UC
161	ANM161	Leyland PD2/30 East Lancs. L27/28R	1960 – 1970 UC

Fleet No.	Licence No.	Type	New – Withdrawn
162	ANM162	Leyland PD2/30 East Lancs. L27/28R	1960 – 1970 UC
163	ANM163	Dennis Loline11 East Lancs. H35/28F	1960 – 1970 UC
164	ANM164	Dennis Loline11 East Lancs. H35/28F	1960 –1970 UC
165	EMJ165	Albion LR7 East Lancs. H35/30F	1963 – 1970 UC
166	EMJ166	Albion LR7 East Lancs. H35/30F	1963 – 1970 UC
167	EMJ167	Albion LR7 East Lancs. H35/30F	1963 –1970 UC
168	EMJ168	Albion LR7 East Lancs. H35/30F	1963 – 1970 UC
169	EMJ169	Albion LR7 East Lancs. H35/30F	1963 – 1970 UC
170	EMJ170	Albion LR7 East Lancs. H35/30F	1963 – 1970 UC
171	HTM171	Albion LR7 East Lancs. H35/30F	1963 – 1970 UC
172	HTM172	Albion LR7 East Lancs. H35/30F	1963 – 1970 UC
173	HTM173	Albion LR7 East Lancs. H35/30F	1963 –1970 UC
174	HTM174	Albion LR7 East Lancs. H35/30F	1963 – 1970 UC
175	HTM175	Albion LR7 Neepsend H35/30F	1963 – 1970 UC
176	HTM176	Albion LR7 Neepsend H35/30F	1963 – 1970 UC
177	HTM177	Albion LR7 Neepsend H35/30F	1963 – 1970 UC
178	HTM178	Albion LR7 Neepsend H35/30F	1963 – 1970 UC
179	HTM179	Albion LR7 Neepsend H35/30F	1963 – 1970 UC
180	HTM180	Albion LR7 Neepsend H35/30F	1963 – 1970 UC
181	FXD181C	Dennis Loline111 Neepsend H39/30F	1965 – 1970 UC
182	FXD182C	Dennis Loline111 Neepsend H39/30F	1965 – 1970 UC
183	FXD183C	Dennis Loline111 Neepsend H39/30F	1965 – 1970 UC
184	FXD184C	Dennis Loline111 Neepsend H39/30F	1965 – 1970 UC
185	FXD185C	Dennis Loline111 Neepsend H39/30F	1965 – 1970 UC
186	FXD186C	Dennis Loline111 Neepsend H39/30F	1965 – 1970 UC
101	MXD101E	Bristol RELL6L ECW B48D★★	06/67 – 1970 UC
102	MXD102E	Bristol RELL6L ECW B48D	06/67 – 1970 UC
103	MXD103E	Bristol RELL6L ECW B48D	06/1967 – 1970UC
104	MXD104E	Bristol RELL6L ECW B48D	06/67 – 1970 UC

Fleet No.	Licence No.	Type	New – Withdrawn
105	MXD105E	Bristol RELL6L ECW B48D	06/67 – 1970 UC
106	NXE106E	Bristol RELL6L ECW B48D	06/1967 – 1970 UC
107	NXE107E	Bristol RELL6L ECW B48D	1967 – 1970 UC
108	NXE108E	Bristol RELL6L ECW B48D	1967 – 1970 UC
109	NXE109E	Bristol RELL6L ECW B48D	1967 – 1970 UC
110	NXE110F	Bristol RELL6L ECW B48D	1967 – 1970 UC
111	PXE111F	Bristol RELL6L ECW B48D Semi Auto	1968 – 1970 UC
112	PXE112F	Bristol RELL6L ECW B48D Semi Auto	1968 – 1970 UC
113	PXE113G	Bristol RELL6L ECW B48D Semi Auto	1968 – 1970 UC
114	PXE114G	Bristol RELL6L ECW B48D Semi Auto	1968 – 1970 UC
115	PXE115G	Bristol RELL6L ECW B48D Semi Auto	1968 – 1970 UC
116	PXE116G	Bristol RELL6L ECW B48D Semi Auto	1968 – 1970 UC
117	PXE117G	Bristol RELL6L ECW B48D Semi Auto	1968 – 1970 UC
118	PXE118G	Bristol RELL6L ECW B48D Semi Auto	1968 – 1970 UC
119	PXE119G	Bristol RELL6L ECW B48D Semi Auto	1968 – 1970 UC
120	PXE120G	Bristol RELL6L ECW B48D Semi Auto	1968 – 1970 UC
121	UXD121G	Bristol RELL6L ECW B48D Semi Auto	1968 – 1970 UC
122	UXD122G	Bristol RELL6L ECW B48D Semi Auto	1968 – 1970 UC
123	UXD123G	Bristol RELL6L ECW B48D Semi Auto	1968 – 1970 UC
124	UXD124G	Bristol RELL6L ECW B48D Semi Auto	1968 – 1970 UC
125	UXD125G	Bristol RELL6L ECW B48D Semi Auto	1968 – 1970 UC
126	UXD126G	Bristol RELL6L ECW B48D Semi Auto	1968 – 1970 UC
127	UXD127G	Bristol RELL6L ECW B48D Semi Auto★★★	1968 – 1970 UC
128	UXD128G	Bristol RELL6L ECW B48D Semi Auto★★★	1968 – 1970 UC
129	UXD129G	Bristol RELL6L ECW B48D Semi Auto★★★	1968 – 1970 UC
130	UXD130G	Bristol RELL6L ECW B48D Semi Auto★★★	1968 –1970 UC

The five vehicles listed below did not enter service before the UC takeover and were disposed to Eastern Counties Omnibus Co. Nos LHS595–9. They were re-registered WNG 101–5H, and entered service in February 1970. Interestingly they had a different livery of a red roof and lower panels with cream window surrounds and black lining out to the cream relief and black wheels. This livery was not operated in public service.

131	XXE131H	Bristol LHS6P ECW B37F	11/1969	1970 UC
132	XXE132H	Bristol LHS6P ECW B37F	11/1969	1970 UC
133	XXE133H	Bristol LHS6P ECW B37F	11/1969	1970 UC
134	XXE134H	Bristol LHS6P ECW B37F	11/1969	1970 UC
135	XXE135H	Bristol LHS6P ECW B37F	11/1969	1970 UC

Ten vehicles ordered by LCT would have been numbered 136–145. They did not enter service with LCT. The first five were delivered to UC in February 1970, in UC livery.

348	VNV348H	Bristol RELL6G B46D	1970 – 1970 UC
349	VNV349H	Bristol RELL6G B46D	1970 – 1970 UC
350	VNV350H	Bristol RELL6G B46D	1970 –1970 UC
351	VNV351H	Bristol RELL6G B46D	1970 – 1970 UC
352	VNV352H	Bristol RELL6G B46D	1970 – 1970 UC

Denotes:

★	Vehicle replaced by another with the same fleet number.
da	Vehicle withdrawn due to war damage beyond repair.
★★	Re-numbering commenced at 101.
★★★	Stored by LCT, did not enter service.
UC	Transferred to UC fleet in 1970.

A fully detailed fleet list is available from the PSV Circle contained in their publication *PN3*. This publication also contains information on demonstration vehicles, both operated and inspected, and service vehicles owned.

During the early part of the war the fleet sustained heavy bomb damage. Some two dozen Bristol/ECW double-deckers were loaned by ENOC from their Clacton-on-Sea depot as temporary replacements for vehicles damaged by air attacks on the Park Street depot in September 1940.

At the time of publication 184 is thought to still exist in France and is being used as a mobile bank. 129 (UXD 129G) has been saved and is currently undergoing restoration.

APPENDIX 2

FLEET DISPOSAL DETAILS

No.	Withdrawal	Disposal	Details
1	44		Davis, South Mimms Herts (Dealer)
2	08/40	10/40	War damage Aug/Sept. Destroyed at Thurgoods Ware whilst under repair
3	40	05/41	War Dept. 05/41, Nat Fire Service 07/44, France 07/47, Market Weighton, 07/50 scrapped
4	44		Davis, South Mimms, Herts. (Dealer)
5	4/48		Unknown
6	44		Brookmans Park. Herts in garage, later workshop Brunts Coaches Bell Bar, Herts. Scrapped by Moss Mardley Hill Herts
7	44		G. Moss, Mardley Hill Herts Scrapped
8	44		Davis, South Mimms Herts (Dealer)
9	05/45		Davis, South Mimms Herts (Dealer) C.F.G. Southampton (Dealer)
10	05/45	05/45	Davis, South Mimms Herts (Dealer) Roadway Autocar, Barnet Herts, then scrapped
11	05/45	05/45	Davis, South Mimms, Herts (Dealer) Roadway Autocar Barnet, Herts, then scrapped
12	44	05/45	Davis, South Mimms, Herts (Dealer) Roadway Autocar, Barnet Herts then scrapped
13	04/48	06/48	Horton Motor Works, Northampton
14	10/47	10/47	Dismantled for spares by LCT
15	46	11/49	Probably used as towing vehicle until used by Corporation as Mobile Library 11/49 To unknown breaker, scrapped in 1957
16	04/48	04/48	Horton Motor Works, Northampton, later to Carpenter Bishop's Castle
17	40	05/41	To War Dept.
18	46	10/47	Dismantled for spares by LCT
19	40	09/40	War damage Aug/Sept. Destroyed at depot G.E. Moss, Mardley Hill Herts to scrap

No.	Withdrawal	Disposal	Details
20N	9/51		Lansdowne London E11 for fleet Withdrawn 9/52
21N	48	06/48	G. A. Woodman, Baldock, Herts
22N	08/40	10/40	War damage Aug/Sept. Destroyed at Thurgoods, Ware whilst under repair
24N	09/51	01/52	Lansdowne, London E11 for fleet. Withdrawn 9/52
25N	09/51	01/52	Lansdowne, London E11. for fleet Withdrawn 9/52
27N	52	06/52	Towing vehicle, cut down in 1953. Operated on Trade licence 682BM until 12/53/66 D. Higgs & Son Ltd, Barnsley Yorks for scrap
29N	09/40	09/40	War damage. Believed not returned to service, likely used as spares by LCT
30	04/48	06/49	Davis, South Mimms, Herts (Dealer) scrapped
31	04/48	06/49	Davis, South Mimms, Herts (Dealer) scrapped
32	04/48	08/48	Turner, Luton
33	04/48	10/48	Flettons, Water Eaton
34	04/48	06/49	Davis, South Mimms, Herts (Dealer) scrapped
35	04/48	06/48	Leader, London E15
36	04/48	06/49	Davis, South Mimms, Herts (Dealer) scrapped
37	46	10/47	Dismantled for spares by LCT.
38	04/48	06/49	Davis, South Mimms, Herts. 04/52 Body only in yard at Lewisham, London S.E.13
39	04/48	06/49	Davis, South Mimms, Herts (Dealer)
41	50	04/50	Davis, South Mimms, Herts. 04/51 Showman's vehicle
42	50	04/50	Davis, South Mimms, Herts (Dealer)
43	46	10/47	Dismantled for spares by LCT
44	46	10/47	Dismantled for spares by LCT
45	50	04/50	Davis, South Mimms, Herts (Dealer)
46	09/51	01/52	Lansdowne, London E11 for fleet. Withdrawn 9/52
47	50	4/50	Davis, South Mimms, Herts (Dealer) 04/51 Showman's vehicle. Appeared regularly at Wormwood Scrubs fair until 1961
48	50	04/50	Davis, South Mimms, Herts (Dealer)
49	09/51	01/52	Lansdowne, London E 11 for fleet. Withdrawn 9/52
50	49		Mossman, Bury Farm Caddington, Luton. Possible living accom. Then a hen house. 8/69 derelict at Caddington. 01/70 Broken up
51	54	06/54	Bird. Stratford-upon-Avon. (Dealer)
52	50	04/50	Davis, South Mimms, Herts (Dealer)
53	54	06/54	Bird, Stratford-upon-Avon. (Dealer)
54	09/51	01/52	Lansdowne, London E 11 for fleet. Withdrawn 1/53
55	09/51	01/52	Lansdowne, London E 11 for fleet. Withdrawn 1/53
56	9/51	01/52	Lansdowne, London E 11 for fleet. Withdrawn 9/52
57	50	01/53	Edwards, London Colney, Herts. Spares then scrapped
58	53	12/53	Billy Smart's Circus as Showman's vehicle
59	50	04/50	Davis, South Mimms, Herts. (Dealer)
60	04/48	06/48	A&E Palmer Motors, Luton. 06/48 for sales at Romford, Essex. 1951 with A&F Cox Rainham, Essex (non PSV)

No.	Withdrawal	Disposal	Details
61	06/53	08/53	Benhill Machinery & Equip. Co. Then exported
62	06/53	08/53	Benhill Machinery & Equip. Co. Then exported
63	52	08/53	Benhill Machinery & Equip. Co. Then exported
64	53	12/53	Billy Smart's Circus as Showman's vehicle
65	50	1/53	Edwards, London Colney, Herts, spares then scrapped
66	53	12/53	Billy Smart's Circus, Showman's vehicle
67	50	01/53	Edwards, London Colney, Herts, spares then scrapped
68	52	08/53	Bexhill, London, then exported possibly to Spain
69	50	01/53	Edwards, London Colney, Herts, spares then scrapped
70	54	06/54	Bird, Stratford-upon-Avon (Dealer)
71	54	06/54	Bird. Stratford-upon-Avon (Dealer)
72	54	06/54	Bird, Stratford-upon-Avon. (Dealer)
73	54	06/54	Bird, Stratford-upon-Avon. (Dealer)
74	57	04/58	Groves. London SW19 scrapped
75	57	04/58	Groves, London SW19 scrapped
76	53	12/53	Billy Smart's Circus for use as power unit
77	53	12/53	Billy Smart's Circus for use as power unit
78	53	12/53	Billy Smart's Circus for use as power unit
79	53	12/53	Billy Smart's Circus for use as power unit
80	56	12/56	W. North, Leeds. Yorks. (Dealer)
81	56	12/56	W. North, Leeds. Yorks. (Dealer) 12/57 Blamires, Bradford, then scrapped
82	53	12/53	Carney (Dealer) Rugeley, Staffs
83	57	04/58	Groves, London SW19 (Dealer) scrapped
84	56	12/56	W. North, Leeds. Yorks. (Dealer)
85	56	12/56	W. North, Leeds. Yorks. (Dealer)
86	56	12/56	W. North, Leeds. Yorks. (Dealer) 05/57 Blamires, Bradford, then scrapped
87	56	12/56	W North, Leeds. Yorks. (Dealer) 04/57 Blamires, Bradford, then scrapped
88	60	02/61	H. Smith, Luton. (Dealer) scrapped
89N	60	02/61	H. Smith, Luton. (Dealer) scrapped
90N	60	02/61	H. Smith, Luton. (Dealer) scrapped
91N	60	02/61	H. Smith, Luton. (Dealer) scrapped
92	63	01/63	Thompson, Luton (Coal Merchant) presumed scrapped
93	63	01/64	Thompson, Luton (Coal Merchant) presumed scrapped
94	63	01/64	Thompson, Luton (Coal Merchant) presumed scrapped
95	63	11/63	Thompson, Luton (Coal Merchant) scrapped at Harts Motors, Markyate, Herts, gone by 06/64
96	63	11/63	Thompson, Luton (Coal Merchant) presumed scrapped
97	63	12/63	Thompson, Luton (Coal Merchant) scrapped at Harts Motors, Markyate, Herts, gone by 06/64
98	63	11/63	Thompson, Luton (Coal Merchant) presumed scrapped
99	63	01/64	Thompson, Luton (Coal Merchant) presumed scrapped
100	65	01/66	D. Higgs & Son Ltd, Monk Bretton, Barnsley, Yorks Presumed scrapped
101	65	01/66	D. Higgs & Son Ltd, Monk Bretton, Barnsley, Yorks Presumed scrapped
102	65	01/66	D. Higgs & Son Ltd, Monk Bretton, Barnsley, Yorks Presumed scrapped
103	65	01/66	D. Higgs & Son Ltd, Monk Bretton, Barnsley, Yorks Presumed scrapped
104	66	05/66	D. Higgs & Son Ltd, Monk Bretton, Barnsley, Yorks Presumed scrapped

No.	Withdrawal	Disposal	Details
105	65	01/66	D. Higgs & Son Ltd, Monk Bretton, Barnsley, Yorks Presumed scrapped
106	66	05/66	D. Higgs & Son Ltd, Monk Bretton, Barnsley, Yorks Presumed scrapped
107	66	05/66	D. Higgs & Son Ltd, Monk Bretton, Barnsley, Yorks Presumed scrapped
108	66	05/66	D. Higgs & Son Ltd, Monk Bretton, Barnsley, Yorks Presumed scrapped
109	63	05/66	Broken for spares by LCT. Then as scrap to D. Higgs & Son, Monk Bretton, Barnsley, Yorks
110	63	05/66	Broken for spares by LCT. Then as scrap to D. Higgs & Son, Monk Bretton, Barnsley, Yorks
111	63	05/66	12/63 Fitted with towing gear. Pvt licence until 4/66 on Trade plate B93 CXD. Spares by LCT. Then as scrap to D. Higgs & Son
112	66	02/67	Hartwood Finance Ltd, Barnsley Yorks. Presumed scrapped
113	66	02/67	Hartwood Finance Ltd, Barnsley Yorks. Presumed scrapped
114	66	02/67	Hartwood Finance Ltd, Barnsley Yorks. Presumed scrapped
115	66	02/67	10/66 Fitted with towing gear. Trade plate B93 CXD whilst 123 being re-painted. 02/67 Hartwood Fin. Ltd Presumed scrapped
116	67	11/69	07/67 Pvt. Licence. Used as LCT Training Bus. To unknown dealer at Hockliffe, Beds
117	66	02/67	Hartwood Finance Ltd, Barnsley Yorks. Presumed scrapped
118	67	08/67	W. North, Sherburn in Elmet, Yorks. (Dealer) Later works bus for 'Double Two Shirts' Wakefield, Yorks. Still in service 10/69.
119	67	08/67	W. North, Sherburn in Elmet, Yorks. (Dealer) Later Rigby, Patricroft, Lancs. For fleet. Likely not used and returned to North for scrap
120	67	08/67	W. North, Sherburn in Elmet, Yorks. (Dealer) Later Rigby, Patricroft, Lancs. For fleet. Likely not used and returned to North for scrap
121	67	08/67	W. North, Sherburn in Elmet, Yorks. (Dealer) Scrapped 1/68
122	66	02/67	Hartwood Finance Ltd, Barnsley, Yorks. Presumed scrapped.
123	66	11/69	4/66 Fitted with towing gear. Pvt. Licence. 11/69 to unknown dealer at Hockliffe, Beds
124	67	09/67	W. North Sherburn in Elmet Yorks. (Dealer)
125	67	09/67	W. North Sherburn in Elmet Yorks (Dealer) 11/67 R Costain (Contractor) Later in Oldham, Lancs with Dept. of Emp. at building site
126	67	09/67	W. North Sherburn in Elmet Yorks (Dealer) 11/67 R Costain (Contractor)
127	67	11/67	W. North Sherburn in Elmet Yorks (Dealer) 11/67 R Costain (Contractor) Later Walker, Hexthorpe. Yorks
128	67	09/67	W. North Sherburn in Elmet Yorks. (Dealer)
129	68	68	Not known
130	69	69	Not known
131	68	12/68	Unknown breaker, scrapped
132	69	69	Believed to Martin, Weaverham, Cheshire (Dealer)
133	69	69	Believed to Martin, Weaverham, Cheshire (Dealer)
134	69	69	Believed to Martin, Weaverham, Cheshire (Dealer)

No.	Withdrawal	Disposal	Details
135	69	69	Martin, Weaverham, Cheshire (Dealer)
136	68	12/68	By 05/69 Whites Coaches St Albans, Herts. Still in service 02/70
137	69	69	Believed to Martin, Weaverham, Cheshire (Dealer) Later Mersey Docks and Harbour Board Birkenhead.
138	68	68	Not known

All remaining vehicles in the fleet numbered 139–186 and 101–135 passed to UC in January 1970.

DISPOSAL DETAILS OF OTHER VEHICLES BOUGHT INTO THE FLEET FROM OTHER OPERATORS:

Origin	LC No.	W/D	Disposal	Reg.	Type	Details
Bluebird	N/O	33		TM5480	Chevrolet	Unknown
Bluebird	N/O	06/34		TM3446	Dennis G	G.C. Cook (London dealer)
Bluebird	N/O	34		TP7959	Dennis G	see note (a)
Bluebird	N/O	34		UL5919	Dennis G	see note: (a)
Union Jack	N/O	34		RO9518	Dennis G	G.C. Cook (London dealer, scrapped)
Bluebird	20	02/35	35	UM6401	Dennis E	see note (b)
Bluebird	21	07/34	35	TM5909	Dennis EV	see note (b)
Bluebird	22	07/34	35	MT7868	Dennis ES	see note (b)
Bluebird	23	03/39	03/39	TM3739	Dennis ES	Luton Civil Defence, then Luton Electricity Undertaking
Union Jack	24	12/37	04/38	RO8252	Dennis E	Morrell, Leeds, (Dealer)
Bluebird	25	04/37	04/38	TM5910	Dennis EV	Morrell, Leeds, (Dealer)
Union Jack	26	12/38	03/39	TM6084	Dennis EV	Luton Civil Defence, then Luton Electricity Undertaking
Union Jack	27	07/37	04/38	JK210	Dennis ES	Morrell, Leeds, (Dealer)
Bluebird	28	09/47	6/49	TM9539	Dennis Lance	W. Davis, South Mimms, Herts. (Dealer) scrapped.
Bluebird	29	3/34	35	VM6402	Dennis E	see note (b)
Union Jack	40	09/38	04/39	MJ459	Dennis ES	Luton ARP (Civil Defence) Mobile Unit. Then Showman's engine by 1950.
ENOC	89	65	01/66	JEV419	Bristol K5G.L27/28R	Higgs & Son, Monk Bretton, Barnsley, Yorks. Engine exported Hong Kong
ENOC	90	65	01/66	JEV426	Bristol K5G L27/28R	Higgs & Son, Monk Bretton, Barnsley, Yorks. Engine exported Hong Kong
ENOC	91	65	01/66	JEV416	Bristol K5G.L27/28R	Higgs & Son, Monk Bretton, Barnsley, Yorks. Engine exported Hong Kong

(a) One of these two vehicles was sold to Union Jack for £90 in December 1933. The other was sold in January 1934 to Union Jack. Both vehicles were with ENOC by December 1936 although not used. They were then passed to Searle, Colchester (Dealer) and scrapped.

(b) G. Cook London (Dealer) July 1934. All four buses to Gosport and Fareham Omnibus Co. No.20 withdrawn 1947 then Showman's engine until April 1952. No.21 withdrawn 1950, damaged by fire at Hoeford 1957, scrapped 1962. No.22 withdrawn 1940. Fareham ARP as ambulance, later Showman's engine at Reading. Last licensed 1950. No.29 withdrawn by GFOC in 1943, then a Showman's engine, seen at Epsom in May 1952.

Key   N   denotes re-allocated number.

            N/O   denotes LCT did not operate vehicle in public service.

FLEET NOTES

Acquired vehicles that operated:

20   Originally Manchester Corporation No.141
21   Ex XL No.12
22   Originally with W.D. Beaumont, Enfield. Middx
24   Originally E. Prentice & Son (Chiltern Bus Co.) Tring. To Union Jack in 1932
25   Ex XL No.14
26   Originally Hinds & Savage, Luton, then Bluebird, then Union Jack
27   Originally Twines, Eastbourne, Sussex, then Southdown No.392 in 1930, later Union Jack
29   Originally Manchester Corporation No.142
40   Chassis number is quoted as 17952 (Claimed by South Wales Transport WN4452) it is assumed that this vehicle had chassis 17592 new c.1928. A thirty-two-seat chassis was owned by England in October 1932. It is believed that this was fitted subsequently.

Notes on some acquired vehicles that did not operate:

RO9518   Originally E. Prentice & Son (Chiltern Bus Co.) Tring. Came to Union Jack from Red Rose, Wendover, Bucks January 1930
TM3446   Originally H.J. Witherington, Toddington, Beds, then Union Jack

Notes on newly acquired vehicles:

- 1–5 and 15 had route boxes consisting of a single line only front and rear. Number stencils fitted later.
- 6–14 had a large single rectangular box front and rear. A shallower blind was fitted later. Number stencils fitted later.
- 16 and 17 quoted also as B32R. Possibly up seated. Destination displays as 1–5.
- 18 and 19 and 30–36 had a large rectangular destination box front and rear with radiused corners. Possibly had shallow blinds from new. Certainly did so later. Also had the route number stencil holder in the front upper-deck nearside window.
- All Daimler double-deck buses incorporated off and nearside drop gangways on upper-deck with three seats in between.
- 20, 21, 22 and 29 replaced the previously acquired vehicles with these fleet numbers.
- 20, 21, 22, 45, 46–49 and 54–56 had destination boxes similar to earlier deliveries, but with separate route apertures fitted on the nearside of the front destination. 29 and 37 had destination displays as 30–36 or as 38 onwards.

- 38, 39, 41–44 and 50–53, 57–59 and 61–70 had separate destination and route apertures with route number box sited centrally over the destination front and rear. Some of these were later modified to single boxes to take rectangular blinds.
- 45 also quoted as B39F.
- 50 had no rear destination box when withdrawn.
- 71–75 had full utility bodywork, chassis from pre-war stock unfrozen. Rear upper-deck emergency exits not glazed when new. 74 was glazed in later years. 75's upper rear window was divided into three, originally intended for Hicks of Braintree. Destination displays on all were a single rectangular box at the front only. The destination surround on 71–74 was of the type found on BET fleets. In 1951 the top and bottom were blocked out to display a later type of blind. Also, side boxes of the new size were fitted. On 75 the top of the box only was blocked out and a side box fitted.
- 76–83 were full utility vehicles with unglazed upper-deck exits. Glazed exit later fitted to 80 and transferred to 83 on withdrawal of 80. Destination display was single rectangular box at front only. 76–81's size was reduced in 1951 by fitting a blank at the top of the box, as on 75. Also, in 1951 82 and 83 had a complete new aperture to the size of the new blind. Again in 1951 80, 81 and 83 received side boxes to the size of the new display.
- 84–85 and 86–87 were full utility with wooden slatted seats. Rear upper exits were all glazed upon delivery. Destination boxes, consisted of single rectangular displays at front and side. The only modifications during their service were re-seating the lower saloons in moquette. 85 had a black-painted radiator shell, during the recent years at least.
- 88–91 had post-war Weymann bodies (non utility). Destination boxes were single rectangular boxes front and side with a central number box at rear.
- 92–99 had a single rectangular box destination display, front and side, with radiused corners and central number box at rear. Brockhouse turbo transmissions were removed in 1953 and constant mesh gearboxes fitted by AEC at depot in Southall in order to overcome heavy fuel consumption.
- 100–108 had destination boxes, as did 92–99. These were modified in 1951 by adding a metal strip to the top of the boxes for reduced size blinds. New rear blinds were fitted in 1964 due to service re-numbering. All had holders for boards on the bulkhead, as did 109–111. 100 and 102–108 had their side boxes painted out and subsequently replaced by a new panel in 1963. 101 retained its box. 106 received a rubber surround to the front box.
- 109–111 were delivered in Luton livery to Chesterfield specification. Single shallow rectangular destination boxes at front and side. Small central number blind at rear.
- 112–123's destination displays were single rectangular boxes front and side with central a number box at rear. Modified by fitting metal strip to top of box in 1951 to display reduced size blind. New rear blinds fitted in 1964. 112, 113, 115–120, 122 and 123 had side boxes painted out and subsequently replaced by new panels in 1963. 114 and 121 retained side boxes. 114 received a rubber surround to rear box in 1962. 123 was treated, as was 114 in 1966. All had reg. no. on off-side front mudguard. Rear number plate was carried under glass below lower-deck window. This applied to all subsequent Leyland Titans. All had chrome radiator shells except two, which had red-painted shells. These tended to be swapped between vehicles. By 1960 117 and 118 had the painted shells. Sometimes aluminium shells from later Titans 124–138 batch found their way onto these vehicles, one such case was 115 in 10/63.
- 124–138 had large three-aperture displays front and rear with destination, route number and intermediate screens below on off side and near side respectively. The rear display protruded from the panelling. New route number blinds were fitted in 08/64. All were supplied with aluminium radiator shells. In 10/63 133 received a chrome shell from the 112–123 batch. It had reverted back by 10/67, 126 was fitted with 'Auster' opening vents in the front upper and lower-deck windows in about 1955. 134 had flashing indicators fitted around 1966.
- 139–147 had similar displays to the 124–138 batch, except that the rear display was flush, not protruding. 139, 141–144 and 147 had later type panels fitted to the 'tin fronts' to the same design as 148 onwards. 139–143 had flashing indicators fitted c.1966. 140 had its upper front dome re-built with smaller windows and no vent after colliding with the footbridge at Luton Railway Station.
- 148–152 were as the 139–147 batches, but with updated 'tin fronts'. Blinds were the same as previous batch. Flashing indicators were fitted c.1966.

- 153–157 were the first 8ft-wide vehicles received at Luton. Indicators already fitted at delivery. Fibreglass domes. Blinds as previous batch.
- 158–162's displays were similar to the previous batch, but with radiused corners. 160 had its rear destination display removed in December 1968 and replaced with a flush panel used for advertising. 160 also had its window between saloon and cab modified for driver tuition by November 1969.
- 163–164 were the first forward entrance vehicles in the fleet. 164 had been an exhibit at 1960 Commercial Motor Show at Earls Court, fitted with wheel trims, later removed. Delivered with similar style displays as previous but rear displays were removed and replaced with a flush panel in late 1967 used for advertising.
- 165–180's air suspension was replaced by coil springs starting in 1969. Triangular dark glass windows by the lower landing were removed and panelled during 1967. Destination displays were as 163–164.
- 181–186's destination blinds continued to show separate destination, intermediate and route number, but within a single rectangular aperture with corners radiused front and rear. Rear displays were panelled over late in 1967. 181 carried an advertisement over its destination display before being panelled over! These vehicles carried chassis numbers, which indicated that they had semi-automatic gearboxes.
- 101–130's destination displays were the standard 'Tilling' two-aperture style, showing a single line destination and a route number on the offside of the ECW three-track type. All the ECW one-man-operated buses had front and central air-operated doors. 101–110 had standard four-speed synchromesh gearboxes. 111–130 had semi-automatic boxes. 122 was severely damaged by fire at its rear end whilst in service on route 29 on 17 August 1969. The vehicle was sent for investigation to Leyland. By November 1969 it had been returned to Gordon Coachworks, Bilton Way, Luton, for body repair, completed February 1970.

APPENDIX 4

STATISTICS

Year	Annual Revenue	Passengers Carried	Mileage	Profit/Loss	Basis of calculation
1932/33	N/A	4,685,899	420,000	N/A	Actual
1933/34	N/A	6,200,000	950,000	N/A	Estimated
1934/35	N/A	9,500,000	1,000,000	N/A	Estimated
1935/36	N/A	10,500,000	1,200,000	-81	Estimated
1936/37	N/A	12,000,000	1,300,000	N/A	Estimated
1937/38	N/A	13,000,000	1,600,000	N/A	Estimated
1938/39	N/A	13,500,000	1,650,000	N/A	Estimated
1939/40	N/A	14,000,000	1,475,000	N/A	Estimated
1940/41	N/A	14,500,000	1,450,000	N/A	Estimated
1941/42	N/A	17,500,000	1,600,000	N/A	Estimated
1942/43	N/A	18,500,000	1,600,000	N/A	Estimated
1943/44	N/A	17,500,000	1,550,000	N/A	Estimated
1944/45	N/A	19,500,000	1,600,000	N/A	Estimated
1945/46	N/A	N/A	N/A	N/A	War Time Statistics withheld
1946/47	168,724	N/A	N/A	8371	Actual
1947/48	175,510	24,402,950	2,141,358	11649	Actual 8mths grossed up
1948/49	199,021	23,523,679	2,156,962	−35568	Actual
1949/50	212,579	21,180,005	2,159,253	N/A	Ave. 4 wks seasonally adj.
1950/51	215,064	22,117,545	2,080,948	N/A	Ave 12 wks gross
1951/52	239,899	25,266,936	1,875,904	N/A	Ave 11 wks gross
1952/53	228,583	24,749,176	1,881,670	−74029	Ave 15 wks gross seasonally adj.
1953/54	257,915	27,608,132	1,994,541	N/A	Ave 11 wks gross seasonally adj.
1954/55	278,455	27,685,463	1,961,148	N/A	Ave 3 wks gross seasonally adj.
1955/56	284,684	27,440,419	1,964,700	N/A	Ave 20 wks gross seasonally adj.
1956/57	321,760	29,804,089	2,044,631	N/A	Ave 5 wks gross seasonally adj.
1957/58	324,015	31,060,819	2,148,466	1676	Actual
1958/59	370,185	N/A	2,741,000	N/A	Ave 22 wks gross seasonally adj.

Year	Annual Revenue	Passengers Carried	Mileage	Profit/Loss	Basis of calculation
1959/60	392,741	N/A	N/A	N/A	Ave 13 wks gross seasonally adj.
1960/61	393,510	N/A	N/A	N/A	Ave 15 wks gross seasonally adj.
1961/62	437,123	36,098,163	2,501,877	N/A	Ave 8 wks gross seasonally adj.
1962/63	472,087	N/A	N/A	N/A	Ave 13 wks gross seasonally adj.
1963/64	493,847	N/A	N/A	N/A	Ave 19 wks gross seasonally adj.
1964/65	550,569	N/A	N/A	N/A	Ave 12 wks gross seasonally adj.
1965/66	579,920	N/A	N/A	N/A	Ave 10 wks gross seasonally adj.
1966/67	N/A	N/A	N/A	N/A	
1967/68	N/A	N/A	N/A	−154,786	Actual
1968/69	N/A	N/A	N/A	−226,000	Actual
1969/70	N/A	N/A	N/A	N/A	No records known

Note: Statistics not recorded during war period at request of Ministry of Information.

KNOWN COORDINATED ROUTE REVENUE STATISTICS

Month	Receipts		Mileage		Tickets Issued		
Date	LC	ENOC	LC	ENOC	LC & ENOC	Ave Ticket	Revenue per mile
31/03/1952	4,413	5,126	38,082	37,722	493,927	0.02	0.13
28/02/1953	4,589	4,760	38,045	38,044	487,991	0.02	0.12
30/04/1953	5,160	5,159	38,279	38,115	549,555	0.02	0.14
01/04/1954	5,449	5,446	38,082	38,280	536,810	0.02	0.14
01/04/1955	5,537	5,615	38,085	38,895	540,714	0.02	0.14
01/09/1956	6,262	5,993	39,717	39,693	598,545	0.02	0.15
01/06/1962	8,432	7,909	50,835	51,011	677,451	0.02	0.16

APPENDIX 5

SUMMARY OF LCT SERVICES OPERATING IN 1939

		Frequency	Origin
1	Seymour Avenue–Pembroke Avenue★	Daily	Tram
2	Waller Avenue–Vauxhall Works	M – F	(Contract 1932)
3	Electrolux Works–Seymour Avenue	M – F	(Stage 6.32)
4	Park Square–Lewsey Road/Chaul End Lane	Daily	Tram
5	Library–Dunstable (town hall)	Daily	ex-UJ
6	Library–Dunstable (via Houghton Regis)	Daily	ex-XL
7	Cutenhoe Road–Fountans Road	Daily	Tram
8	Farley Hill–Biscot Mill	M – F	Intro. 5.33
9	Russell Rise–Hart Lane (Circular)	Daily	Intro. 9.32
10	Library–Round Green (Peak only as 11)	M – F	Tram
11	Library–Stopsley	Daily	Intro. 4.33
12	Library–Round Green (via Colin Road)	Daily	ex-BB
13	Library–Leagrave (via Biscot Road)	M – F	ex-BB
14	Bridge Street–Biscot Mill (via Biscot Road)	Daily	ex-BB
15	Bridge Street–Biscot Mill (via Old Bedford Road)	Sun.	ex-BB
16	Bridge Street–Bramingham Turn	M – F	ex-BB
17	Richmond Hill–Vauxhall Works	M – F	Intro. 33
18	Farley Hill–Vauxhall Works	M – F	ex-UJ 1.34 (former contract)
19	Library–Dunstable (via Leagrave)	Sun	ex-BB
20	Biscot Mill–Vauxhall Works	M – F	Intro. 1.3.36
21	Stopsley–Vauxhall Works/Airport (As a result of inadequate service by ENOC)	M – F	Intro. 1.37
22	Park Square–Chaul End Lane	M – F	Intro. 3.37
23	Park Square–Airport	Daily	Intro. 6.4.37
24	Cutenhoe Road–Vauxhall Works	M – F	Intro. 1.38

★Pine Street renamed as Pembroke Avenue

APPENDIX 6

LUTON AND DISTRICT TRANSPORT SERVICES FOLLOWING COORDINATION 02/01/49

LCT 1	Cutenhoe Road–Hockwell Ring
LCT1A	Cutenhoe Road–Leagrave (Sugar Loaf)
LCT 2	Discontinued
LCT 3	Discontinued
EN 3	Whipsnade–Dunstable–Bedford
EN 3B	Dunstable–Toddington
LCT 4	Stopsley Green–Skimpot, Lewsey Road. (New cross town service incorporating EN55 and LCT 4)
LCT 5	Luton (Library)–Dunstable
LCT 6	Luton (Library)–Houghton Regis–Dunstable
LCT 7	Cutenhoe Road–Fountains Road
LCT 8	Whipperley Way–Bradgers Hill Road
LCT 9	Russell Rise–Biscot Mill
LCT 10	Discontinued
LCT 11	Warren Road–Stopsley (Rochester Avenue) (New cross town service incorporating EN 63, part of 52D and LCT 11)
LCT 11A	Warren Road–Stopsley (Green) via Hart Lane and Ashcroft Road.
LCT 12	Luton (Library)–Round Green
EN 12	Luton–Shefford
EN 12A	Luton–Pegsdon
LCT 13	Vauxhall Works–Biscot Mill
LCT 14	Discontinued
EN 14	Luton (Williamson Street)–Meppershall
EN 14A	Luton (Williamson Street)–Bramingham Lane–Pegsdon
LCT 15	Vauxhall Works–Whipperley Ring (introduced 2/1/49)
LCT 16	Discontinued, duplicated route EN 14A to Bramingham Lane
EN 16	Luton–Aylesbury
LCT 17	Vauxhall Works–Richmond Hill
LCT 18	Re-numbered LCT 15
EN 18	Luton (Williamson Street)–Wing
EN 18A	Luton (Williamson Street)–Leighton Buzzard
EN 18B	Luton (Williamson Street)–Tilsworth–Leighton Buzzard Station

LCT 19	Discontinued duplicated by EN 53
LCT 20	Re-numbered LCT 13
EN 20	Luton (Williamson Street)–Ampthill–Bedford
EN 20A	Luton (Williamson Street)–Wilstead–Bedford
EN 20B	Luton (Williamson Street)–Clophill–Pulloxhill
EN 20D	Luton (Williamson Street)–Clophill–Flitwick
LCT 21	Discontinued combined with ENOC 52D
LCT 22	Discontinued
LCT 23	Luton (Park Square)–Airport
LCT 24	Cutenhoe Road–Vauxhall Works
EN 52	Luton (Park Square)–Hitchin–Letchworth–Baldock
EN 52B	Luton (Park Square)–Hitchin–Stotfold
LCT and EN 52D	Round Green–Chaul End Lane, plus special peaks to Vauxhall Ministry of Transportors
EN 53	Luton (Williamson Street)–Dunstable
EN 53A	Luton (Williamson Street)–Dunstable Station
LCT and EN 53B	Luton (LMR) Station–Dunstable–Whipsnade Zoo (Operated with LCT)
EN 53C	Luton (Williamson Street–Dunstable (Hambling Place)
EN 54	Luton (LMR) Station–Leagrave
LCT and EN 56	Luton–Limbury
LCT and EN 56A	Luton (Vauxhall– Limbury
LCT and EN 57	Luton–Leagrave (Hockwell Ring)
EN 59	Luton (LMR) Station–Sundon
EN 66	Luton (LMR) Station–Bletchley

LUTON AND DISTRICT TRANSPORT SERVICES AT HANDOVER 01/70

6	LCT	Luton (Library Bus Station)–Dunstable (Kensworth Lane)
11	LCT	Warren Road–Stopsley (Wandon Close)
12	UC	Round Green–Roman Road/Oakley Road
13	Shared	Vauxhall Works–Limbury (Biscot Mill)
14	UC	Luton (Library Bus Station)–Bramingham Lane
15	LCT	Vauxhall Works–Farley Hill Est. (Whipperley Ring)
17	LCT	Vauxhall Works–Richmond Hill
23	UC	Sundon (Skefko)–Toddington
24	LCT	Vauxhall Works–Cutenhoe Road
25	LCT	Cutenhoe Road–Hockwell Ring
27	LCT	Cutenhoe Road–Fountains Road
28	LCT	Round Green–Whipperley Ring
29	LCT	Luton Airport–Town Centre–Priestleys (One Way)
30	LCT	Priestleys–Town Centre–Limbury (Icknield Way) (One Way)
31	LCT	Luton Airport–Town Centre–Limbury (Icknield Way (One Way)
32	LCT	Luton Airport–Luton (Park Square)
33	LCT	Luton (Williamson Street)–Limbury (Biscot Mill)
41	UC	Luton (Library Bus Station)–Leagrave–Dunstable (Hambling Place)
42	UC	Luton (Library Bus Station)–Dunstable (Hambling Place)
43	Shared	Luton (Library Bus Station)–Whipsnade
45	LCT	Stopsley (Crowland Road)–Dunstable (Katherine Drive)
46	LCT	Dunstable Town Centre–Dunstable (Croft Estate)
50	UC	Luton (LMR Station)–Sundon Park (Fourth Ave)
51	UC	Luton (LMR Station)–Sundon Park (Mendip Way)
52	UC	Luton (LMR Station)–Sundon Village
54	UC	Luton (LMR Station)–Toddington
55	UC	Luton (Melson Street)–Limbury Meads
56	UC	Luton (Melson Street)–Limbury mead Estate
56A	UC	Luton (Vauxhall)–Limbury Mead Estate
57	UC	Luton (LMR Station)–Hockwell Ring
58	UC	Luton (LMR Station)–Lewsey Estate (Wheatfield Road)
61	UC	Luton (Library Bus Station)–Aylesbury
64	UC	Luton (LMR Station)–Toddington
66	UC	Luton (Library Bus Station)–Bletchley
68	UC	Luton (Library Bus Station)–Hockliffe–Leighton Buzzard
69	UC	Luton (Library Bus Station)–Eddlesborough–Leighton Buzzard
70	UC	Luton (Library Bus Station)–Tilsworth–Leighton Buzzard Station
71	UC	Luton (Library Bus Station)–Dunstable
94	UC	Luton (Library Bus Station)–Hitchin–Baldock

95	UC	Luton (Library Bus Station)–Baldock via Letchworth Works Road
96	UC	Luton (Library Bus Station)–Stotfold via Norton
97	UC	Luton (Library Bus Station)–Stotfold via Fairfield Hospital
98	UC	Luton (Library Bus Station)–Stotfold via Letchworth Works Road
142	UC	Luton (Library Bus Station)–Ampthill–Bedford
143	UC	Luton (Library Bus Station)–Wilstead–Bedford
144	UC	Luton (Library Bus Station)–Pulloxhill–Clophill
145	UC	Luton (Library Bus Station)–Flitwick–Clophill

APPENDIX 8

ROUTE INFORMATION

Route 1   **LCT and LDT**

1932   Luton (Bailey Street)–Beechwood Road
06/33   Extended to Bailey Street–Waller Avenue
06/36   Proposed ext. from Bailey Street to Cutenhoe Road/Seymour Avenue junction
09/36   Extension from Bailey Street to Cutenhoe Road/Seymour Avenue junction
11/36   Proposed ext. from Waller Avenue to Pembroke Avenue
1939   Seymour Avenue–Pembroke Avenue (Pine Street renamed as Pembroke Avenue)
11/47   Proposal to extend from Pembroke Avenue to Hockwell Ring (Agreed after ENOC objection, but to share with ENOC 57)
05/48   Service 1A introduced as alternative to Hockwell Ring terminus
02/01/49   Extended to Cutenhoe Road from Seymour Avenue
02/01/49   Extended to 'Sugar Loaf' on Leagrave Estate from Pembroke Avenue
08/51   Some peak journeys terminated at Vauxhall Works instead of Cutenhoe Road
01/10/61   1A extended to Emerald Road/Lewsey Farm Estate
26/01/64   1A extended from Emerald Road to Hereford Road, Lewsey Farm Estate
23/04/67   Re-numbered 25
23/04/67   1A discontinued

Route 2   **LCT**

1932   Beechwood Road–Vauxhall (Contract)
05/06/32   Became (Peak Stage) otherwise as Route 1
06/33   (Extended from Beechwood Road to Waller Avenue–Vauxhall Works
06/36   Proposed extension from Bailey Street to Cutenhoe Road/Seymour Ave junction
09/36   Extended as above
02/01/49   Discontinued

Route 3   **LCT**

1932   Luton (Bailey Street)–Electrolux (Contract)
06/32   Stage: Luton (Bailey Street)–Electrolux
01/34   Luton (Park Square)–Chaul End Lane (Dropped 07/34 see service 4)
06/36   Proposed ext. from Park Square to Cutenhoe Road/Seymour Avenue junction
09/36   Extended as above
1939   Electrolux Works – Luton Seymour Avenue
1940   Proposed ext. from Electrolux to 'Sugar Loaf' declined
09/49   Discontinued and run as 1A works via Electrolux at peak times

Route 4   **LCT and LDT**

1932   Luton (Bailey Street)–Beechwood Road

23/3/33	Luton (Park Square)–Beechwood Road
01/34	Permission granted for extension to Chaul End Lane
07/34	Extension from Beechwood Road to Chaul End Lane implemented
11/36	Proposed part service to be extended from Chaul End Lane to Lewsey Road
03/37	Harry Nutall keen to extend part service to Skimpot
04/37	Traffic Comm. Requested revised turning arrangements in Lewsey Road
06/37	Part service Luton (Park Square)–Lewsey Road introduced. (Every third journey) along with part service to Skimpot
10/47	Proposed cross-town service to Stopsley Green via Ashcroft Road from Skimpot/ Chaul End Lane/Lewsey Road. Part service from Park Square to be shared with ENOC 55 on a temporary basis pending continued negotiations
09/49	Above arrangement taken into coordination agreement absorbing ENOC 55 into service 4
08/51	Some Peak journeys terminated at Vauxhall Motors
09/51	Alternate journeys between Stopsley–Lewsey Road and Skimpot (formally Chaul End Lane)
09/11/52	Route change to operate along a new section of Ashcroft Road instead of Williton Road and Yeovil Road to avoid difficult turns on a camber
05/60	Extension from Stopsley Green to Crowland Road implemented
01/10/61	Skimpot terminus extended to Dunstable Hadrian Avenue, Lewsey Road terminus extended to Dunstable (Hadrian Avenue)
23/04/67	Re-numbered: 44 Stopsley (Crowland Road)–Skimpot–Dunstable (Katherine Drive)
23/04/67	Re-numbered: 45 Stopsley (Crowland Road)–Lewsey Road–Dunstable (Katherine Drive)

Route 5 LCT & LDT

23/3/32	Luton (Library)–Dunstable (Town Hall)
09/11/33	Introduction of Double-deck buses on this service
02/38	Application to extend 18.05 journey from Dunstable to Waterlow Works
05/01/42	Luton (Library)–Dunstable (Kensworth Lane) at Peak
16/09/51	Discontinued
01/10/61	Re-introduced: Luton (Library)–Houghton Regis (Tithe Farm Estate)
23/04/67	Discontinued

Route 6 LCT and LDT

23/03/32	Luton (Library)–Houghton Regis–Dunstable (Great North Road)
09/11/33	Introduction of Double-deck buses on this service
10/36	Dunstable Council request for ext. to Great North Road to McManus Est. Refused
04/38	18.05 journey extended from Dunstable to Waterlow Works. (As applied for route 5)
04/38	Request by Dunstable Council to extend within Dunstable
12/38	Traffic Comm. urges extension to Kensworth Lane Dunstable
12/39	Traffic Comm. refused extension within Dunstable
01/42	Traffic Comm. agrees extension to Dunstable (Kensworth Lane) at Peak
12/55	Extended to Dunstable (Kensworth Lane)
23/04/67	Luton terminus changed to Library Road Bus Station
	Later Luton Bus Station

Route 7 LCT and LDT

01/3/32	Luton (Bailey Street)- Stockingstone Road
11/33	Application to extend to Ludlow Avenue declined
18/01/34	Extension to New Bedford Road Greyhound track granted for use when suitable
04/10/35	Extended from Stockingstone Road to Culverhouse Road/Street Augustines Avenue junction. Extended from Bailey Street to Cutenhoe Road/London Road

11/36	Proposed Terminus to be changed from Culverhouse/Street Augustines Avenue to Fountains Road
1938	Extension to Fountains Road implemented.
	Remained single-deck operation until the Second World War probably due to overhanging trees in New Bedford Road
12/40	Terminus at London Road changed to turn at Cutenhoe Road via West Hill Road
07/02/53	Extension from Fountains Road to Biscot Mill at Peak only
05/53	Proposed extension from Fountains Road to Biscot Mill
01/10/61	Extended from Fountains Road to Calverton Road/Watermead Road (Limbury Mead Estate)
26/01/64	Terminus reverted to Fountains Road
23/04/67	Re-numbered 27

Route 8   **LCT and LDT**

05/33	Farley Hill–Stockingstone Road
1935	Proposal to extend to Biscot Mill from Stockingstone Road
26/01/47	Sunday service introduced to replace service 15
05/48	Caddington PC request ext to Caddington. Declined as it infringed on LTB territory
02/01/49	Extended into Farley Hill Estate to Whipperley Way and from Stockinstone Road to Bradgers Hill Road
03/49	Farley Hill residents request extension into estate when roads are made up
01/51	Proposal to extend from Whipperley Way further into estate at Whipperley Ring
16/09/51	Re-routed from Bradgers Hill Road to Round Green (to compensate for loss of route 12)
1952	Proposal for Farley Hill terminus to be extended to Priestleys
25/11/52	Experimental hourly shuttle service at peaks Town Centre (Bridge Street) to Farley Hill (Russell Rise)
05/53	Above frequency of shuttle increased
26/01/64	Re-numbered 28

Route 9   **LCT and LDT**

12/10/32	Russell Rise–Hart Lane (Clockwise Circular)
05/36	Proposal to operate service in both directions. Not introduced at this time
12/37	Application for Sunday service declined
06/38	ENOC objected to introduction of Sunday service
02/46	Sunday service introduced
02/01/49	Circular discontinued. Became Russell Rise–Biscot Mill
01/51	Proposal to extend from Russell Rise to Priestleys/Longcroft Road junction. Later agreed
09/51	Service in two sections: Luton (George Street)–Biscot Mill and Luton (Bridge Street)–Russell Rise
1952	Proposed extension to Meyrick Avenue rejected as road unsuitable
05/53	Permission given to operate between Biscot Mill and Longcroft Road/Priestleys to commence 01/11/53
01/10/53	Permission withdrawn. Public meeting 20/10/53
01/11/53	Agreed but did not commence. Biscot Mill–Longcroft Road/Priestleys. (This would reduce pressure on service 8)
07/02/55	Extended from Russell Rise to Priestleys and shortened from Biscot Mill to Old Bedford Road/Greenhill Avenue. Biscot Mill Peaks only
08/56	Petition by residents to extend from Greenhill Ave to Bradgers Hill Road declined
09/56	Decided that at a future date to link with route 23 and extend to Bradgers Hill Road
01/02/58	Extended from Old Bedford Road to Bradgers Hill Road
01/02/58	Service 9: Priestleys–Town Centre–Airport–Bradgers Hill Road
01/02/58	Service 9A introduced: Bradgers Hill Road–Town Centre–Airport
26/1/64	9 and 9A extended to Icknield Way, Limbury from Bradgers Hill Road
23/4/67	Re-organised and re-numbered as 29 and 30

Route 10   LCT

17/04/32	Luton (Library)–Round Green
01/04/33	Became off-peak service otherwise as service 11 on daily basis
01/01/49	Discontinued

Route 11   LCT and LDT

01/04/33	As service 10 but extended at peak: Luton (Library)–Round Green–Stopsley Green. Service ran in conjunction with ENOC service 55
06/04/37	Proposal for a Stopsley terminus extension to Stapleford Road. (No change occurred until post-war)
06/37	Proposal to extend Stopsley terminus to Ashcroft Road/Turners Road junction with increased frequency. Not implemented
10/37	Former proposal to extend to Ashcroft Road changed to Chesford Road. (No change occurred as Putteridge Road remained unmade)
02/39	Petition from residents of Ashcroft Road for extension of service to meet their needs, declined
1939	Extension agreed to Rochester Avenue via Putteridge Road when road made up. (Not implemented until 1947)
03/47	Proposal for alternative route from Luton (Library)–Stopsley Green via Crawley Green Road and Ashcroft Road. Due to ENOC objections application stalled. 08/47
11/47	11A introduced to fulfil above, but remained Luton(Library)–Stopsley Green
11/47	Extension from Stopsely Green to Rochester Avenue (11 only) ENOC 52D also extended from Stopsley Green to Rochester Avenue
02/01/49	Changed to cross town service from Dallow Road/Warren Road–Stopsley (Rochester Avenue) incorporating ENOC 63, LCT 11 and the Round Green–Stopsley Green portion of ENOC 52D
16/09/51	11A discontinued
06/59	Proposed extension at Stopsley to Wandon Close. Became subject of public enquiry held. 4/2/60. Objections overruled, permission granted
1/10/61	Extension to Stopsley (Wandon Close) implemented. Other information suggests implemented 5/60

Route 12   LCT and LDT

12/03/32	Luton (Manchester Square)–Colin Road
12/35	Extended from Colin Road to Round Green terminus
02/39	Round Green terminus moved across the road to Stockingstone Road junction
01/47	Proposal to extend to Bloomfield Avenue from Round Green. Proposal considered until 08/47, and then declined
06/47	Luton terminus changed from Manchester Square to Luton Library
16/09/51	Discontinued. Part replaced by 52D and 8 (jointly operated between ENOC and LCT)
26/01/64	Number re introduced. Old 52D route re-numbered 12
26/01/64	Round Green – Oakley Road/Roman Road
26/01/64	Also peak Vauxhall Works–Round Green–Oakley Road/Roman Road
07/68	Round Green–Hockwell Ring via Selbourne Road instead of Leagrave Road

Route 13   LCT and LDT

23/03/32	Luton (Manchester Square)–Biscot Mill–Leagrave (Sugar Loaf)
02/36	Sunday service introduced to counter ENOC service
06/47	Luton terminus changed from Manchester Square to Luton Library
02/01/49	Works service only at peak. Vauxhall Motors–Town Centre–Biscot Mill. Former LCT 20
1972	Discontinued. Replaced by peak service on 32 via Old Bedford Road to Vauxhall

Route 14   LCT and LDT

23/03/32	Luton (Manchester Square)–Biscot Mill
04/33	Probably converted to double-deck operation
02/36	Increased schedule on Saturdays to counter ENOC service
11/36	Approval for extension from Biscot Mill to Culverhouse Road. (Not introduced until post-war as roads unmade) (Manchester Square now called Bridge Street)
01/01/49	Discontinued
06/50	Petition for reinstatement of service
09/51	ENOC operated services 14 and 14A. 14 Luton (Bridge Street)–Biscot Mill–Meppershall. (Certain 14A services terminated at Bramingham Lane) others continued to Pegsdon
01/10/61	14A discontinued
23/04/67	Luton terminus became Library Road Bus Station
26/04/70	Luton terminus became Luton Bus Station

Route 15   LCT and LDT

23/03/32	Luton (Manchester Square)–Old Bedford Road–Biscot Mill (Sunday only)
26/01/47	Discontinued replaced by service 8
02/01/49	Re introduced as works service: Vauxhall Motors–Farley Hill (Whipperley Way) Former 15 amalgamated with 18
16/9/1951	Extended to Whipperley Way

Route 16   LCT

23/03/32	Luton (Manchester Square)–Bramingham Lane (M - F)
18/1/34	Application agreed to include New Bedford Road Greyhound Track on race days
01/01/49	Discontinued

Route 17   LCT and LDT

11/33	Introduced stage service Richmond Hill–Vauxhall Works (former Contract only service)

Route 18   LCT

11/33	Application to convert to stage service Vauxhall–Richmond Hill
01/34	Introduced. Albert Road–Vauxhall Works (M - F)
11/36	Extended from Albert Road to Farley Hill (Whitehill Avenue)
04/37	Farley Hill terminus changed from Whitehill Avenue to Stockwood Park gates
01/01/49	Discontinued

Route 19   LCT

23/03/32	Luton (Manchester Square)–Leagrave – Dunstable (Sunday only)
02/36	Revised service times to counter ENOC
06/47	Luton terminus changed to Luton Library
01/01/49	Discontinued

Route 20   LCT

12/35	Service proposed Biscot Mill–Vauxhall Works (M - F) peaks
04/36	Introduced
01/01/49	Discontinued. Another report suggests discontinued 1939

Route 21   LCT

12/36	Service proposed Stopsley Green–Vauxhall Motors (M - F) peaks
01/37	Introduced
11/04/40	Extension from Vauxhall Motors to airport
02/43	Attempts to divert airport journey via Eaton Valley Road blocked by private developer
01/01/49	Discontinued

Route 22   LCT
11/36   Service proposed Luton (Park Square)–Chaul End Lane (M – F)
06/04/37   Introduced
01/01/49   Discontinued

Route 23   LCT and LDT
18/01/37   Proposed Luton (Park Square)–Eaton Green Road (Airport Boundary) daily peak
06/04/37   Introduced (Using new Bedford Road WTB fleet No.60)
05/37   Extended from Park Square to LMS Station
09/37   Proposal to extend from borough boundary to airport
10/38   Extension to airport implemented. (Single-deck until 1946)
12/39   Proposed additional summer evening services May–Sept and weekend afternoons.
12/46   Full service introduced
11/49   Proposal to move Luton terminus from Park Square to a more central point in the
            town centre. (This did not proceed)
09/56   Decided to link this service with route 9 at some future date
01/02/58   Re-routed via Crawley Green Road. (Conflicting report states 05/11/54)
01/02/58   23A introduced taking old route 23
23/04/67   23 and 23A discontinued. No changed to 32
23/04/67   Number re-introduced: Skefko Works, Toddington

Route 24   LCT and LDT
06/37   Proposed Cutenhoe Road–Vauxhall Motors (M – F)
01/38   Introduced

Route 25   LCT and LDT
23/04/67   As former route 1

Route 27   LDT
23/04/67   Formally service 7. Cutenhoe Road–Fountains Road
07/68   Cutenhoe Road–Fountains Road shortened to operate Luton (Park Square)–
            Fountains Road

Route 28   LDT
02/01/64   Formally route 8: round Green–Farley Hill (Whipperley Ring)

Route 29   LDT
            Airport Circular: LMR Station–Airport
23/04/67   Introduced as one way service to replace service 9: Airport–Town Centre–
            Priestleys
07/68   Re-organised as: Airport–Town Centre–Priestleys. (Both ways)

Route 30   LDT
23/04/67   Introduced as one way service to replace service 9: Priestleys–Town Centre–Limbury
            (Icknield Road)
70/68   Discontinued. Now service No.29

Route 31   LDT
23/04/67   Introduced to replace service 9A
23/04/67   Airport–Town Centre–Limbury (Icknield Road) One way only
07/68   Discontinued. Now service No.29
07/68   No. re-used. New route 31 Airport–Luton (LMR) Station

Route 32   LDT
23/04/67   Introduced; to replace 23. Luton (Park Square)–Airport (Circular route)

Route 33   **LDT**
23/04/67   Introduced: Luton (Williamson Street)–Biscot Mill (Peak only)
1968   Discontinued

Route 41   **LDT**
23/04/67   Formally co-ordinated ENOC service 53 on Sundays only. Luton (Library Bus Station)–Dunstable (Hambling Place) via Leagrave

Route 42   **LDT**
23/04/67   Formally coordinated ENOC service 53A. Luton (Library Bus Station)–Dunstable (Hambling Place) Timetable co-ordinated with those routes applicable to Aylesbury and Leighton Buzzard Road. Sundays to 'Rifleman' (Dunstable Downs) Peaks to Kensworth Lane, French's Avenue and AC Delco.
07/68   Timetable co-ordinated with route to Aylesbury & Leighton Buzzard Road

Route 43   **LDT**
23/04/67   Formally Co-ordinated ENOC service 53B. Luton (LMR) Station–Whipsnade Zoo

Route 44   **LDT**
23/04/67   Formally service 4: Stopsley (Crowland Road)–Skimpot–Dunstable (Katherine Drive)

Route 45   **LDT**
23/04/67   Formally service 4: Stopsley (Crowland Road)–Lewsey Road–Dunstable. (Katherine Drive) and (Wheatfield Ave) alternately.

Route 46   **LDT**
23/04/67   Dunstable Town Centre service–Katherine Drive

Route 50   **LDT**
23/04/67   Introduced: Luton (LMR) Station–Sundon Park

Route 51   **LDT**
23/04/67   Introduced: Luton (LMR) Station–Sundon (Mendip Way)
   Replaced 59A
26/04/70   Luton (Bus Station)

Route 52   **LDT**
   Number used by ENOC/UCOC Luton–Hitchin–Letchworth–Norton–Baldock
26/01/64   Number no longer used by UCOC. Became 94, 95.
23/04/67   Re-introduced: Luton (LMR) Station–Sundon Village
   Replaced 59
26/04/70   Luton (Bus Station)

Route 52B   **LDT**
   Number used by ENOC/UCOC Luton–Hitchin–Letchworth–Norton–Stotfold
26/01/64   No longer used by UCOC. Became 96, 97 and 98

Route 52D   **LDT**
09/51   Chaul End Lane–Park Square–Round Green with various peaks to Vauxhall Motors, Airport and Stopsley Rochester Avenue instead of Round Green
01/10/61   Regular service terminus extended from Chaul End Lane to Oakley Road
26/01/64   Re-numbered 12

Route 53   **LDT**
23/04/67   Introduced: Luton (Library)–Sundon Park–Toddington

Route 53A   **LDT**
                  Luton (Williamson Street) Dunstable (Station)
16/09/51   Changed to Dunstable (Hambling
                  Place) peak to Kensworth Lane (Empire Rubber) Sundays (Rifleman)
                  Dunstable Downs
12/55   All to Dunstable (Ashcroft) peaks to French's Avenue
01/56   Peak also to AC Delco.
23/04/67   Re-numbered 42

Route 53B   **LDT**
06/47   Introduced: Luton (LMR) Station–Whipsnade Zoo
23/04/67   Re-numbered 43

Route 53C   **LDT**
                  Luton (Williamson Street)–Dunstable (Hambling Place)
16/09/51   Discontinued

Route 54   **LDT**
06/47   Luton (LMR) Station–Leagrave (Anstee Road)–Toddington
09/51   Peak only beyond Anstee Road
28/04/67   Luton (LMR) Station–Toddington

Route 55   **LDT**
26/01/64   Introduced: Luton (Waller Street)–Limbury Mead Estate) Calverton Road/
                  Watermead Road)
23/04/67   Luton (Melson Street)–Limbury Mead Estate
07/68   Luton Bus Station–Limbury Mead Estate

Route 56   **LDT**
09/51   Luton (Park Square)–Limbury (Biscot Mill)
07/02/55   Luton (Waller Street)
01/02/58   Alternate journeys to Runfold Road and Leyburn Road
01/10/61   Extended to Leyburn Road (Runfold Estate)
23/04/67   Luton (Melson Street)
07/68   Luton Bus Station–Limbury Mead Estate

Route 56A   **ENOC and LDT**
09/45   Vauxhall Motors–Cutenhoe Road–Limbury (Bishopsgate
                  Road)

Route 57   **ENOC and LDT**
06/47   Luton (LMR) Station–Leagrave (Sugar Loaf)
09/05/48   changed to Leagrave (Hockwell Ring)
                  Luton (LMR) Station–Marsh Farm Estate
07/68   Luton Bus Station–Marsh Farm Estate

Route 58   **LDT**
23/04/67   Introduced: Luton (LMR) Station–Lewsey Farm Estate (Wheatfield Road)
07/68   Luton Bus Station–Lewsey Farm Estate

Route 59   **ENOC and LDT**
06/47   Luton (LMR) Station–Sundon
09/51   Certain services to Sundon (Fourth Avenue)

01/10/61   Extended from Fourth Avenue to Grampian Way
23/04/67   Re-numbered 52

Route 59A   LDT
01/10/61   Introduced: Luton (LMR) Station–Sundon (Mendip Way)
23/04/67   Re-numbered 51

Route 61   LDT
26/01/64   Introduced: Former ENOC service 16. Luton (Williamson Street)–Aylesbury
26/04/67   Luton (Library Bus Station)

Route 63   ENOC
2/1/49   Former ENOC service Luton (Alma Street)–Dallow Road incorporated within LDT service 11

Route 64   LDT
26/01/64   Introduced: Luton (LMR) Station–Toddington

Route 65   LDT
1960   Introduced: Luton (LMR) Station–Hockliffe–Woburn Sands
23/04/67   Discontinued: Ended with an announcement in a holiday leaflet

Route 66   LDT
              Originally an ENOC route Luton–Dunstable–Fenny Stratford Road–Bletchley Station
1974   Discontinued

Route 68   LDT
26/01/64   Introduced: Luton (Williamson Street)–Hockliffe–Leighton Buzzard Road. Former ENOC 18
23/04/67   Luton (Library Bus Station)

Route 69   LDT
26/01/64   Introduced: Luton (Williamson Street)–Eddlesborough–Leighton Buzzard Road
23/04/67   Luton (Library Road Bus Station)

Route 70   LDT
26/01/64   Introduced: Luton (Williamson Street)–Tilsworth–Leighton Buzzard Road. Former ENOC 18B
23/04/67   Luton (Library Bus Station)

Route 71   LDT
26/01/64   Introduced: Luton (Williamson Street)–Dunstable, Former ENOC 18A
23/04/67   Luton (Library Bus Station)

Route 94   LDT
26/01/64   Introduced: Luton (Park Square)–Hitchin–Baldock. Former ENOC 52
23/04/67   Luton (Library Bus Station)

Route 95   LDT
26/01/64   Introduced: Luton (Park Square)–Hitchin–Letchworth Works–Baldock Former ENOC
23/04/67   Luton (Library Bus Station)

Route 96   **LDT**

26/01/64   Introduced: Luton (Park Square)–Hitchin–Stotfold–via Norton. Former ENOC

23/04/67   Luton (Library Bus Station)

Route 97   **LDT**

26/01/64   Introduced: Luton (Park Square)–Hitchin–Fairfield–Stotfold. Former ENOC

23/04/67   Luton (Library Bus Station)

Route 98   **LDT**

26/01/64   Introduced: Luton (Park Square)–Hitchin–Letchworth Works. Norton–Stotfold. (Former ENOC

23/04/67   Luton (Library Bus Station)

Other Notes of interest.

01/37   Proposed new service by LCT Dunstable Road (Kingsway) and Biscot Mill, ENOC objected

06/37   Proposed new service by LCT Dallow Road–Round Green dropped due to narrow road on Waller Avenue bridge

09/38   LCT proposal to divert services and introduce new circular service to serve Somerset Avenue; but the steep turn from Crawley Green Road into Somerset Avenue was considered unsuitable

APPENDIX 9

ROUTE PLANS

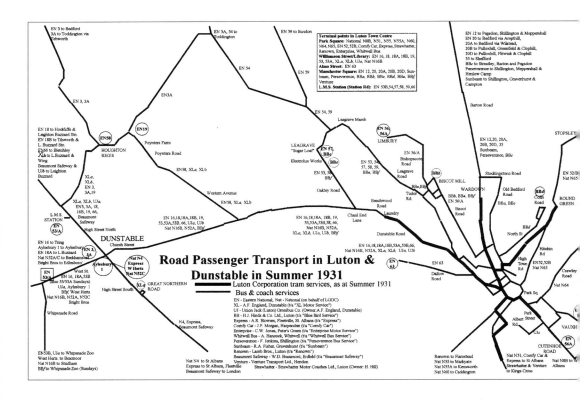

Terminal points in Luton Town Centre
Park Square: National N8B, N51, N55, N55A, N60, N64, N65, EN 52, 52B, Comfy Car, Express, Strawhatter, Renown, Enterprise, Whitwell Bus
Williamson Street/Library: EN 16, 18, 18A, 18B, 19, 53, 53A, XLa, XLb, UJa, Nat N16B
Alma Street: EN 63
Manchester Square: EN 12, 20, 20A, 20B, 20D, Sunbeam, Perseverance, BBa, BBb, BBc, BBd, BBe, BBf, Venture
L.M.S. Station (Station Rd): EN 53B,54,57,58, 59,66

Road Passenger Transport in Luton & Dunstable in Summer 1931

— Luton Corporation tram services, as at Summer 1931
— Bus & coach services

EN - Eastern National, Nat - National (on behalf of LGOC)
XL - A.F. England, Dunstable (t/a "XL Motor Service")
UJ - Union Jack (Luton) Omnibus Co. (Owner:A.F. England, Dunstable)
BB - H.J. Hinds & Co. Ltd., Luton (t/a "Blue Bird Service")
Express - A.R. Blowers, Fleetville, St. Albans (t/a "Express")
Comfy Car - J.P. Morgan, Harpenden (t/a "Comfy Car")
Enterprise - C.W. Jones, Peter's Green (t/a "Enterprise Motor Service")
Whitwell Bus - A. Hancock, Whitwell (t/a "Whitwell Bus Service")
Perseverance - F. Jenkins, Shillington (t/a "Perseverance Bus Service")
Sunbeam - R.A. Fisher, Gravenhurst (t/a "Sunbeam")
Renown - Lamb Bros., Luton (t/a "Renown")
Beaumont Safeway - W.D. Beaumont, Enfield (t/a "Beaumont Safeway")
Venture - Venture Transport Ltd., Hendon
Strawhatter - Strawhatter Motor Coaches Ltd., Luton (Owner: H. Hill)

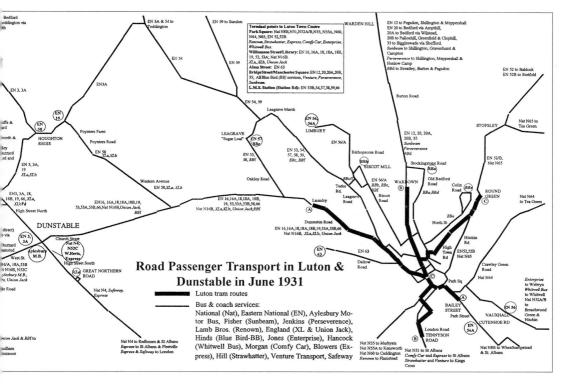

Road Passenger Transport in Luton & Dunstable in June 1931

━━━ Luton tram routes

─── Bus & coach services:
National (Nat), Eastern National (EN), Aylesbury Motor Bus, Fisher (Sunbeam), Jenkins (Perseverence), Lamb Bros. (Renown), England (XL & Union Jack), Hinds (Blue Bird-BB), Jones (Enterprise), Hancock (Whitwell Bus), Morgan (Comfy Car), Blowers (Express), Hill (Strawhatter), Venture Transport, Safeway

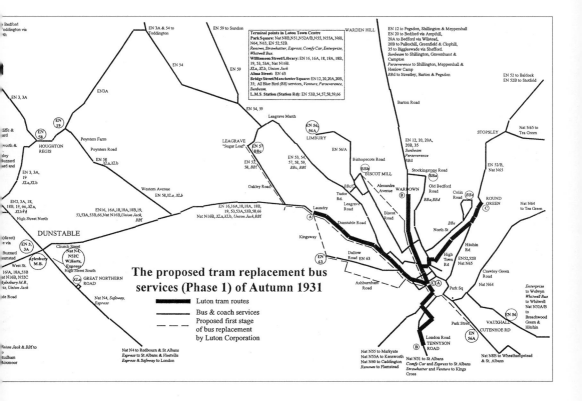

The proposed tram replacement bus services (Phase 1) of Autumn 1931

━━━ Luton tram routes
─── Bus & coach services
– – – Proposed first stage of bus replacement by Luton Corporation

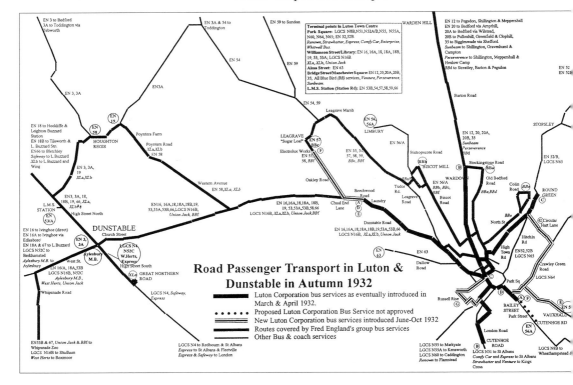

Road Passenger Transport in Luton & Dunstable in Autumn 1932

Luton Corporation bus services as eventually introduced in March & April 1932.
Proposed Luton Corporation Bus Service not approved
New Luton Corporation bus services introduced June-Oct 1932
Routes covered by Fred England's group bus services
Other Bus & coach services

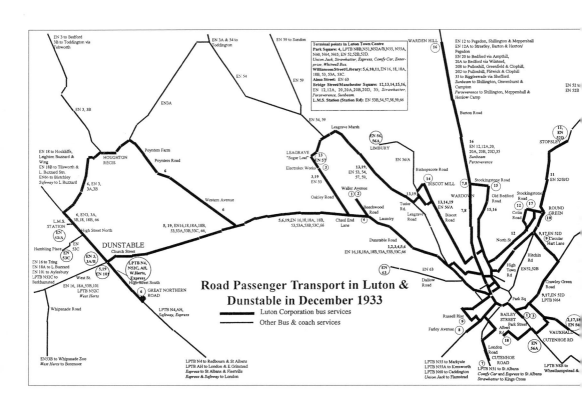

Road Passenger Transport in Luton & Dunstable in December 1933

Luton Corporation bus services
Other Bus & coach services

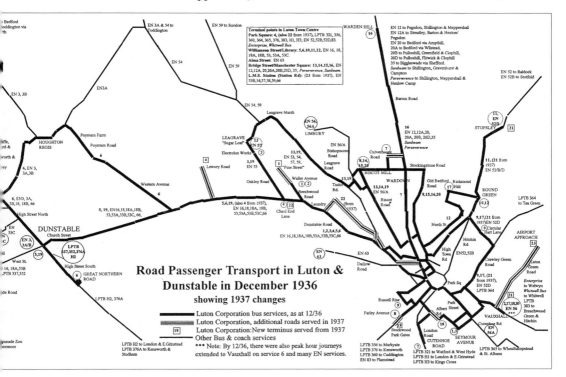

Road Passenger Transport in Luton & Dunstable in December 1936

showing 1937 changes

Terminal points in Luton Town Centre
Park Square: 4, (also 22 from 1937), LPTB 321, 356, 360, 364, 365, 376, 383, H1, H3, EN 52,52B,52D,83.
Enterprise, Whitwell Bus.
Williamson Street/Library: 5,6,10,11,12, EN 16, 18, 18A, 18B, 53, 53A, 53C.
Alma Street: EN 63
Bridge Street/Manchester Square: 13,14,15,16, EN 12,12A,20,20A,20B,20D, 35, *Perseverance, Sunbeam*
L.M.S. Station (Station Rd): (13 from 1937), EN 53B,54,57,58,59,66

——— Luton Corporation bus services, as at 12/36
——— Luton Corporation, additional roads served in 1937
[18] Luton Corporation: New terminus served from 1937
——— Other Bus & coach services
*** Note: By 12/36, there were also peak hour journeys
extended to Vauxhall on service 6 and many EN services.

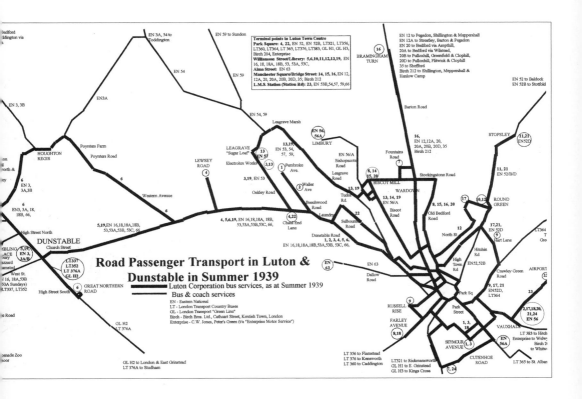

Road Passenger Transport in Luton & Dunstable in Summer 1939

Terminal points in Luton Town Centre
Park Square: 4, 22, EN 52, EN 52B, LT321, LT356, LT360, LT364, LT 365, LT376, LT383, GL H1, GL H3, Birch 204, Enterprise.
Williamson Street/Library: 5,6,10,11,12,13,19, EN 16, 18, 18A, 18B, 53, 53A, 53C.
Alma Street: EN 63
Manchester Square/Bridge Street: 14, 15, 16, EN 12, 12A, 20, 20A, 20B, 20D, 35, Birch 212
L.M.S. Station (Station Rd): 23, EN 53B,54,57, 59,66

——— Luton Corporation bus services, as at Summer 1939
——— Bus & coach services
EN - Eastern National
LT - London Transport Country Buses
GL - London Transport 'Green Line'
Birch - Birch Bros. Ltd., Cathcart Street, Kentish Town, London
Enterprise - C.W. Jones, Peter's Green (t/a 'Enterprise Motor Service')

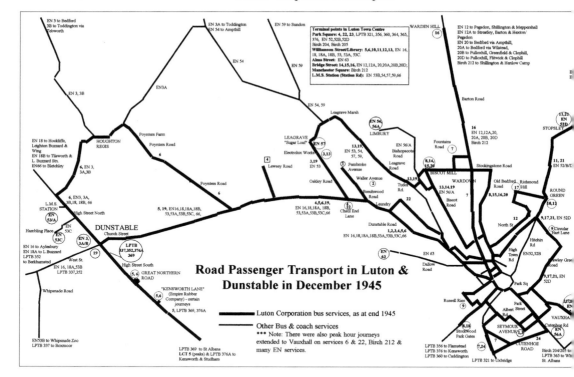

Road Passenger Transport in Luton & Dunstable in December 1945

━━━ Luton Corporation bus services, as at end 1945
─── Other Bus & coach services
*** Note: There were also peak hour journeys extended to Vauxhall on services 6 & 22, Birch 212 & many EN services.

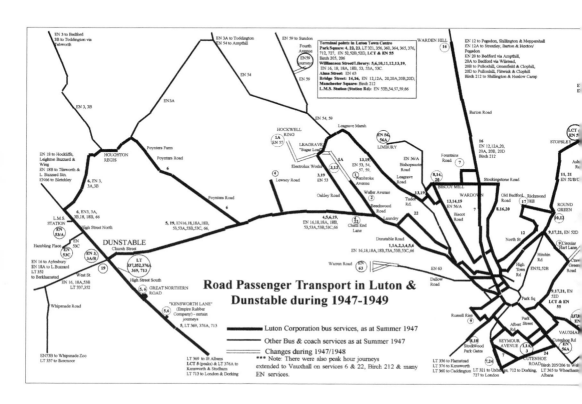

Road Passenger Transport in Luton & Dunstable during 1947-1949

━━━ Luton Corporation bus services, as at Summer 1947
─── Other Bus & coach services as at Summer 1947
Changes during 1947/1948
*** Note: There were also peak hour journeys extended to Vauxhall on services 6 & 22, Birch 212 & many EN services.

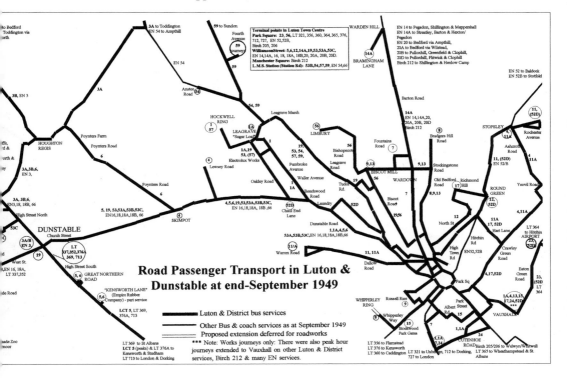

Road Passenger Transport in Luton & Dunstable at end-September 1949

━━━ Luton & District bus services
──── Other Bus & coach services as at September 1949
──── Proposed extension deferred for roadworks

*** Note: Works journeys only: There were also peak hour journeys extended to Vauxhall on other Luton & District services, Birch 212 & many EN services.

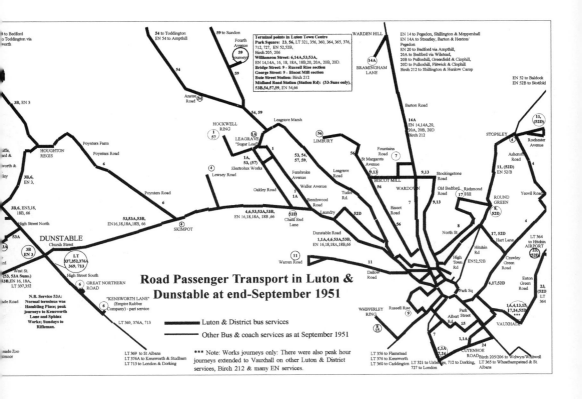

Road Passenger Transport in Luton & Dunstable at end-September 1951

━━━ Luton & District bus services
──── Other Bus & coach services as at September 1951

*** Note: Works journeys only: There were also peak hour journeys extended to Vauxhall on other Luton & District services, Birch 212 & many EN services.

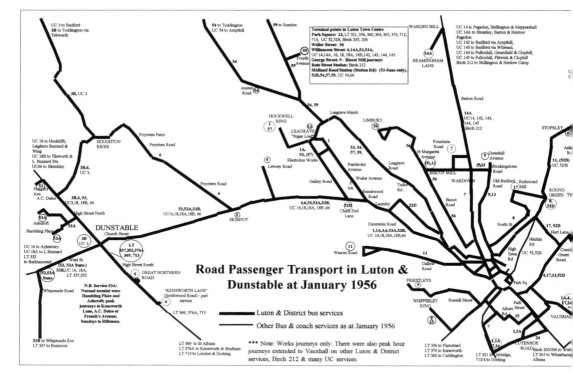

Road Passenger Transport in Luton & Dunstable at January 1956

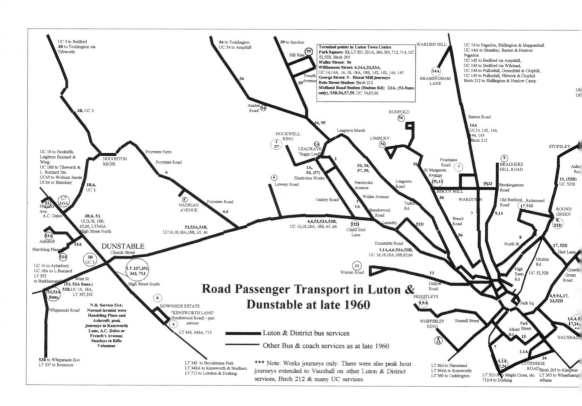

Road Passenger Transport in Luton & Dunstable at late 1960

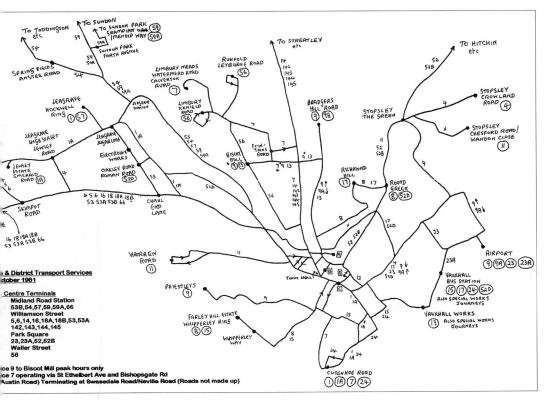

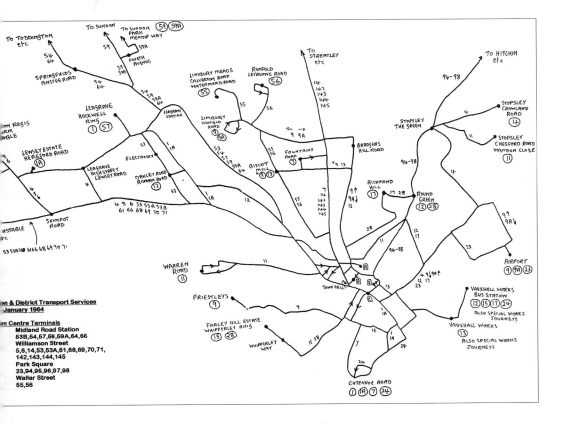

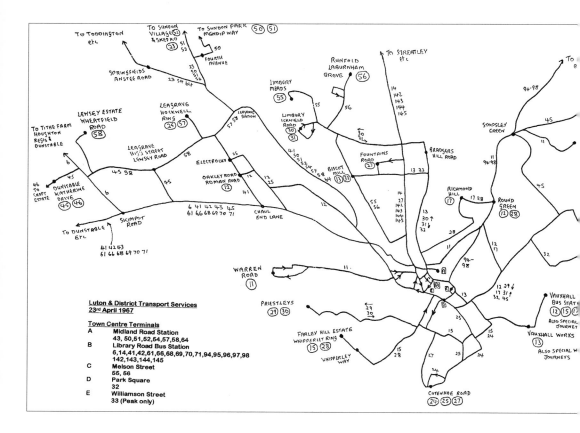

Luton & District Transport Services
23rd April 1967

Town Centre Terminals
A   Midland Road Station
     43, 50,51,52,54,57,58,64
B   Library Road Bus Station
     6,14,41,42,61,66,68,69,70,71,94,95,96,97,98
     142,143,144,145
C   Melson Street
     55, 56
D   Park Square
     32
E   Williamson Street
     33 (Peak only)

APPENDIX 10

LIST OF ILLUSTRATIONS AND ACKNOWLEDGEMENTS

COLOUR SECTION

The book has been researched and worked upon over the past sixteen years when family and work commitments permitted. In recent years my retirement has enabled me to bring the book together. But none of it would have been possible without the help of the following people and organisations:

Graham Smith
PSV Circle
Luton Borough Council (Transport Committee Archives)
Luton Borough Council Museum Service
Luton Borough Council Libraries
Colin Brown
Roger Barton
Alan Parfitt
Graham Ledger
John Cummings

The images used to create the montage of memorabilia in the colour section are from various sources. I am indebted to the following for allowing me to prepare pictures from their collections for use in this publication:

Gerry Seppell-Morris: for a sample of the images from his collection of tickets.
Nigel Adams: for images of LCT tickets and other items.
Luton Cultural Services Trust: for images of LCT timetables and various booklets, (who retain the copyright for these items).

My thanks are given to the following people and organisations for permission to publish their photographs:

8	John Cummings
90, 91, 94	Bristol Vintage Bus Group
38	Colin Brown
C2	C. Carter
1, 2, 3, 5, 6, 7, 10, 25, 64.	Ken Cooper
56, 97, 102, 15, 16, 17, 19,	
23, 27, 28, 29, 35	The late R. Mack (East Pennine Transport Group)
40, 42, 43, 44, 51, 52, 58, 62, 65	Home Counties Newspapers (*Luton News*)
86, 87	G. Mead
18, 36, 39, 41, 47, 48, 50, 80, 82	
85, 88, 92, 93, 95, 96, C4, C5,	
C6, C7, C8, C9, C10, C11, C12,	
C13, C14, C15, C16, C17, C18	Graham Smith.
66, 69, 70, 71, 72, 73, 74, 75	Vauxhall Motors (Archivist)

I am also indebted to Graham Smith for use of his route maps, and to Alan Parfitt for use of three of his route maps.

Permission has been sought for the following pictures. Either the company has indicated that it has no record, or the company or individual cannot be traced:

12	J. Higham
20, 21	Roger Barton
22, 30	Mirror Group (to old to be able to identify as theirs)
26, 31, 37	*Bus & Coach Magazine*
32, 46, 49	A.B. Cross
77, 99	W.J. Haynes

The following pictures are of unknown origin and currently form part of my own collection. Every effort has been made to trace the photographer and seek permission. Although unidentified some may be attributable to the collections of Raymond Simpson, Peter Relf, Solent Slide, Chris Mann and Provincial Bus Promotions – which no longer exists:

2, 9, 11, 13, 14, 33, 34, 45, 53, 54, 55, 57, 61, 63, 67, 68, 76, 78, 79, 81, 83, 84, 89, 98, 100, 101, C1, C3

In respect of all the photographs used, these have been made available from collections built up over a number of years. In many cases the original photographer is not known and to those I wish to acknowledge my gratitude for recording these historical vehicles and events.

Peter Rose
2009

INDEX

Visit our website and discover thousands of other History Press books.

www.thehistorypress.co.uk

M

London Buses After

Capital Transport

The photo above at Waterloo is by John King.

First published 2018

ISBN 978 1 85414 422 5

Published by Capital Transport Publishing Ltd
www.capitaltransport.com

Printed by Parksons Graphics

The front cover photo at Trafalgar Square and
the photo above at Waterloo are by John King.
The title page photo in Strand and the back
cover photo at Morden are by Rob Telford.

INTRODUCTION

There is a certain atmosphere about night photography. It is much easier now, of course, since the advent of digital cameras that record events that would not have been so easily covered with film. Dragging a tripod around, or looking for a suitable flat-topped wall in the right place, was the order of the day with time exposures, and even then, it was mostly guesswork. Many of the trips after dark with my camera produced as many failures as successes, but overall, the process was very rewarding. We take buses for granted in many ways, and don't often think about them running late into the night, and in many cases now, through twenty-four hours. The aim of this book is to illustrate this aspect of operation with many black and white and colour views from the early twentieth century up to the present day. Night routes were comparatively rare in days gone by, but now there are many all over London to serve the public.

I am particularly grateful to my lifelong friend Peter Horner for the opportunity to scan many of his negatives for this volume. We spent many dark evenings in the capital experimenting with night photography during the sixties, sometimes getting soaked and very cold, and some of the fruits of those trips can be seen here.

Mick Webber

A wonderful view at Victoria Station in 1925. The standard buses of the London General fleet are, left to right, NS 1846, K 428, NS 1436, NS 1161, K 570 and B 242. It is probably quite late, as there are not many people visible. The welcoming lit sign for the Underground can be seen on the right at the entrance to the station. A distant sign on the centre left informs the public that the Aerated Bread Company are about to erect a hotel on the site. (Getty Images)

Bus washing in the late 1920s. The NS class buses were gradually fitted with pneumatic tyres from 1928, so this photograph was probably taken in 1926 or 1927. NS 1426 and NS 1378 have worked the 11, and are at rest at Hammersmith garage (latterly Riverside). There are four men working on NS 1426, a very labour-intensive task, and a job that would no doubt last much of the night. (Mick Webber Collection)

The Premier bus company first appeared in their mauve and white livery in 1923, and initially operated from an old aircraft hangar in Cricklewood. The company owned over thirty buses during its lifetime, and GK892 was a Leyland TDI with Duple bodywork built in November 1930. The company was taken over by the LPTB in December 1933. GK892 was given the stock number L 124 and later TD 68 in the new owner's fleet, and was eventually disposed of in January 1939. This scene is in the Strand in the early 1930s. (Mick Webber Collection)

It is a filthy night in Parliament Street. It is December 1924, and a policeman holds the traffic dressed in his waterproof cape. The bus is a Leyland LB from the small fleet of Arthur Raper. He had only three buses at this time carrying the fleet name 'Standard'. He went on to own eight buses in total, but like the rest of the independent operators in London, sold out to the LPTB, which in his case was in November 1933. (Getty Images)

An unidentified ST waits at Edgware Station for its fifty minute journey back to Rayners Lane on route 114 in late 1935. The route had been cut back from Mill Hill in January and extended to Rayners Lane in April. The extension of the Northern Line to Brockley Hill, Elstree South and Bushey Heath never materialised and Edgware was to remain the northern terminus of the line. The Express Dairy shop on the far right is another of the once familiar names to have disappeared from our High Streets. (London Transport Museum)

St George's Hospital had been founded in 1733 on a site at Hyde Park Corner. The hospital was rebuilt and reopened in 1844, and it occupies the background in this view taken in Knightsbridge in 1935. The bus on route 14 is NS 1855, a July 1926 bus that lasted until July 1937. The entrance to Hyde Park Corner underground station is on the right. St George's Hospital was relocated in 1976 to Tooting in south London. (LT Museum)

Left: Aldwych on 30th November 1937. A wet night, and one that marked the end of the road for the NS class. The class had been introduced in May 1923, and saw the London bus progress from solid tyres to pneumatics, and from open top to covered top. NS 1974 is on the short route 166 from the Aldwych to London Bridge, and is on the last journey, terminating at Bank from where it will run dead to its home garage of West Green. The destination board shows a rare use (at the time) of the qualifier 'ONLY' – a feature more widely tried in the early 1950s to no avail.. The bus was first licensed in November 1926, and was eventually sold in May 1938 to Mr Middlemiss. It was one of thirteen sold to this gentleman, who used them to take poor East End children on trips to the countryside. (Getty Images)

Above: The Bank in what looks to be early evening. It is a rotten night, and the pavements glisten. The steps to the Underground look inviting as a way to escape the elements. The scene is probably in the early post-war period, as the buses have no blackout, but the wartime white disc on the rear lower panel of LT 1317 is still in place. The bus is one of the 'Bluebird' LTs built by the London General Omnibus Company in May 1932, and was withdrawn in August 1949.

Sidcup Hill on 4th December 1950. Freezing conditions after heavy snow left the road like an ice rink. One of Sidcup garage's Q type buses is stuck on the ice, and a build-up of buses queue into the distance. This lasted most of the night until gangs with gravel arrived to help the buses gain some grip on the road. The garage staff would have a lot of late arrivals to clean and fuel for the next morning. (Topfoto)

It is early evening in Whitehall and the traffic has thinned after the earlier rush. Park Royal-bodied RT 1583 spent seven years at Holloway between 1950 and 1957, returning there after its first overhaul, with the same body. It is working short to Highgate on the 134. (G.H.F. Atkins)

Above: The short-lived route 5 between Ladbroke Grove and Shepherd's Bush, came to an end on 19th May 1954, and other work would have to be found for the two RTLs from Shepherd's Bush garage that worked it. The last night is depicted here, with a group of enthusiasts posing for the camera. The bus is Park Royal-bodied RTL 1055, new in October 1950. In August it would be transferred to Camberwell. (Alan Cross)

Left: This is Haymarket in the early 1950s. It is a street originally used in Elizabethan times for the sale of fodder and farm produce. All buses are from the RT family, and London Transport has nearly reached its goal of standardisation in the fleet. There are very few private cars in this view, but it is still rather chaotic, and it will be a while before the vehicles will be able to turn left towards Trafalgar Square. The view illustrates the 1950s use of the word 'only' on destination blinds to denote a short working of the route. (Alamy)

Piccadilly Circus with the famous Coca-Cola sign and County Fire Office. This view was taken in the late 1950s, and shows RTL 553 working route 9 from Mortlake garage. The 9 used forty-eight buses from Mortlake and Dalston on the Mon-Fri operation. RTL 553 carried one of the batch of bodies built by Metro-Cammell and numbered RTL 551-1000. They were one quarter of a ton heavier than the other bodies, and were distinguishable by the heavier beading around the centre relief band. (LT Museum)

RTL 560 was a Metro-Cammell bodied bus that kept its original body after its first two overhauls. In this view in Regent Street, it works the 159 from Camberwell garage. (LT Museum)

The splendid early London Transport designed shelters and Underground station at Turnpike Lane feature in this 1959 view. The trolleybus wires in the background will cease to be part of the scene in a couple of years. Weymann-bodied RT 722 from Enfield picks up passengers on route 231 on its way to Alexandra Park from Forty Hill. The bus is picking up at one of the loading islands, originally built for the trams when Turnpike Lane Station opened in September 1932. Last served by trams in February 1938, the islands continued in use by the replacement buses until September 1968. (Alan Cross)

Weymann-bodied RT 4702 from Sidcup garage stands at Orpington Station in March 1959. The 51B was an erratic service running from Eltham Well Hall to Orpington, the bus map of the day stating 'a few journeys only'. Many journeys worked from Sidcup to Orpington only, and the route did not run at all between 9.30am and 4pm or in the evenings. There were only a couple of morning trips on Saturday, and no service on Sundays. (Alan Cross)

Route 229 was the subject of major change from 4th March 1959. The Orpington to Bexleyheath route was extended along the former trolleybus route 698 from Bexleyheath to Woolwich, with rush hour extensions to Victoria Way. These changes had just been implemented when RT 2301, carrying a Park Royal body, was photographed at Abbey Wood, picking up at the stop by the Harrow Inn. The trolleybus turning circle for short working vehicles can be seen in the background. (Alan Cross)

The 7A was a weekday-only service between Acton and London Bridge. There was no service between Oxford Circus and London Bridge in the evenings or Saturday afternoons. This 1959 view shows a busy London Bridge Station forecourt in the rush hour. Middle Row's Park Royal-bodied RTL 480 is ready to depart for Acton at 5.50pm. The bus moved on to Aldenham for overhaul in August 1961. (Alan Cross)

The first Routemaster coach was CRL 4, later RMC 4. It had Leyland running units and was the only Routemaster body to be built by Eastern Coach Works. The vehicle first entered service at Romford on the busy 721 from Brentwood to Aldgate. This spell ended on 29th December 1957, and on 8th January 1958 it commenced work on the 711 from High Wycombe, running through central London to the Surrey town of Reigate. It is seen here outside the garage in April 1958. (Michael Dryhurst)

Brand new RM 621 heads a line-up of Routemasters in Wood Green blinded up to start new route 269, which would replace trolleybuses on the 629 on 26th April 1961. The bus was destined to remain here for over eight years. Wood Green would continue to operate trolleybuses on route 641, until their withdrawal in November 1961. K-class trolleybuses on the left have had their blinds removed and await transfer to Colindale. (Sid Hagerty / 2RT2 Group)

Chislehurst War Memorial on 7th November 1972. This journey has turned short here instead of running on to Petts Wood Station, and is working back to base at Abbey Wood. RT 3982 carries a Park Royal body from 1954. Abbey Wood had this bus from overhaul in November 1966 until May 1977, when it went to Plumstead for a spell until withdrawn in February 1978. (Peter Horner)

A Park Royal body built in 1950 is carried by RTL 529, which is working from Hackney on route 22. The scene is High Holborn on 2nd May 1968 and the RTL class is coming to the end of its service life, the last being withdrawn on the night of 29/30th November. This bus was withdrawn in September, delicensed and stored at Clapton and Poplar, before being sold in February 1970. (Mick Webber)

Uxbridge Station on 13th November 1967. The fog light of Uxbridge's Weymann-bodied RT 2767 threatens to overpower the author's camera as it waits to depart for Hayes Station. The route worked from West Drayton to Hayes, but the West Drayton to Uxbridge section did not operate after 20.30 on Mondays to Fridays. This photograph was taken at about 21.30. (Mick Webber)

This is Liverpool Street, Finsbury Circus in November 1973. Weymann-bodied RT 4281 from Brixton garage is waiting for departure to Streatham on route 133. This bus saw further service at Seven Kings and Palmers Green, before becoming a trainer in February 1978. It was withdrawn a month later. (Peter Horner)

A deserted West Croydon on 5th January 1974. Weymann RT 2052 from Catford waits for passengers at the other end of the 75 for the trip back to Woolwich, which was scheduled to take 1hr 6mins. The bus spent most of 1975 unlicensed before being resurrected to operate from Thornton Heath and Highgate garages before final withdrawal in October 1977. (Peter Horner)

The Crown and Cushion pub in Woolwich was a Victorian building dating from the 1840s. Buses, and earlier, trolleybuses, turned here. It was the terminus for route 75, and shown on the blinds as 'Woolwich Free Ferry'. The pub was demolished in 2008. Catford's RT 4078 carried a Weymann body, and waits for the return to West Croydon on a deserted night. It is 23rd November 1973. The wall on the right is part of the power station originally built here in 1893, and rebuilt in the 1920s. It was demolished in 1978. (Peter Horner)

Victoria Station in the early sixties. RTW 253 from Tottenham on the left is working back to its home garage on the 76, whilst RTL 818 from Gillingham Street loads up on the 52 for Willesden. Like all RTWs, 253 carries a Leyland body, whilst the RTL is bodied by Metro-Cammell. Other vehicles in view are an RTL on the right working the 25 and, lurking in the background, an RM from Cricklewood on route 16. These had been new to the route in 1962.
(Terry Cooper Collection / Mick Webber)

Finsbury Park late one evening in April 1968. RTL 524 carries a Park Royal body and it is working back to Poplar garage on route 106. It is a weekday route that runs from here to Becontree Heath, and the crew are having a chat before leaving. The works for the new Victoria Line can be seen in the background, and the sign proclaims that it would be opening in the autumn of 1968. The section from Walthamstow to Highbury did in fact open in September. (Mick Webber)

Abbey Wood garage in November 1973. The garage had been completely rebuilt after trams were replaced in 1952. RT 4172 is waiting for a last trip on the 180 to Lower Sydenham. It carries a Weymann body from one of the last batch built in 1954. The garage was closed in October 1981 and work transferred to the new Plumstead garage. (Peter Horner)

Route 21 worked from Moorgate to Sidcup garage with variations terminating at London Bridge and New Cross. This working, shown at London Bridge Station, is only going as far as Eltham Well Hall Station. It is 11th November 1972, and RT 922 from New Cross and carrying a Weymann body waits for custom on a very quiet forecourt. (Peter Horner)

Cubitt Town on a very wet night, 4th January 1974. This picture was taken on the last night of RT operation on the 277. The following day one-man-operated DMSs took over and the route was withdrawn between Cubitt Town and Poplar. The bus is Clapton's RT 2782 which was fitted with a Park Royal body dating from 1951. It was delicensed later that month, and then used as a trainer in August. (Peter Horner)

Lewisham, Rennel Street on 8th November 1973. Buses stood here by the Gaumont cinema, which was built in December 1932 and renamed the Odeon in 1962. More recently it has been demolished to make way for a covered shopping centre. Catford's Weymann-bodied RT 4356 has turned short here from Selsdon. (Peter Horner)

Route 77A was a Monday to Friday route from Raynes Park to King's Cross. In February 1969, this working has turned short at Vauxhall, where it stands with others beneath a railway bridge. Vauxhall was the relief point for Stockwell's operations on the 77A and it is possible that the bus is a 'staff cut'. Stockwell's Weymann-bodied RT 300 would soon be transferred to Middle Row and saw service at several more garages until withdrawn in September 1974. (Peter Horner)

The old route 108A that ran through Blackwall Tunnel was re-routed south of the river to run on to Surrey Docks with journeys to London Bridge. February 1969 saw heavy snow falls in the area, and Park Royal-bodied RT 2666 from New Cross is braving the elements at Well Hall. Although the blind shows 'Well Hall roundabout', the crew stopped to have a chat, and decided to run on to Eltham, Southend Crescent. The side road just visible on the right, is Cobbett Road, which is where the bus would have stood, if it had turned short here. (Peter Horner)

It is February 1968, and at this time the 47 between Stamford Hill and Farnborough was a long route running through some very congested areas. It was because of this that the route usually operated in sections, and buses working the whole route were the exception. The section between Stamford Hill and Shoreditch Church did not operate after 19.30 on Mon-Fri, 14.00 on Saturdays and 20.00 on Sundays. Bromley and Catford worked the route with RTs, and Dalston with RTLs. Weymann bodied RTL 1574 waits at Shoreditch Church for its last trip to Bromley garage. It would see a transfer to West Ham in June, before withdrawal in September. (Mick Webber)

Route 109 was introduced between Purley and the Embankment as a replacement for tram routes 16 and 18 on 8th April 1951. Park Royal-bodied RT 2098 waits at the Purley terminus in November 1967, where it shares the stand with Saunders-bodied RT 1857. The original order with Saunders for 250 bodies was increased by a further 50, and the whole batch was delivered between 1948 and 1951. The company was destined to deliver the last London bus body with a roof box. (Mick Webber)

Brixton RT 1658 is at Blackfriars Station on 19th April 1975 on route N87. The N87 followed a figure of 8, crossing over itself at Kennington. It started as route 287 in January 1951 replacing night tram service 1 which followed the same serpentine course across south London. The bus would see further service at Abbey Wood, Plumstead and Barking before finishing its day as a trainer at North Street before withdrawal in 1979. (Eamonn Kentell)

Buses on route 171 for Tottenham stood in Woodside Gardens, as portrayed here by RTL 98 in April 1968.
The conductor leans against a parked Rover with his Gibson ticket machine, looking at the bus. He knows the days
of the RTLs in service are numbered. This bus will be withdrawn in two months' time and 1968 will be the last year
of service for all these vehicles. The journey back to Forest Hill is scheduled to take 90 minutes. (Mick Webber)

Belmont Road, Wallington in November 1972. Metro-Cammell bodied RF 529 is working from Croydon garage, having arrived there after overhaul earlier that month. It has turned short here rather than running on to Hackbridge Corner. When its service days were over, it was exported to a buyer in Mauritius. (Peter Horner)

Hampstead Heath on the night of 25th May 1974. Route N93 was a very irregular service from here to Charing Cross. The first journey left Hampstead at 23.27. There were only six other journeys; two of them worked only as far as Farringdon Street and one from King's Cross to Farringdon only. Holloway (previously Highgate) operated RM 2085 for over five years and at this time it carried the body that had once been on RM 2081. (Peter Horner)

RM 2170 from Turnham Green garage has worked a short to Hammersmith where it stands in May 1974. The full N97 route worked from Turnham Green to Liverpool Street, the first journey leaving Turnham Green at 23.43, and the last at 5.34. Riverside garage can be seen in the distance on the left. Turnham Green garage closed in May 1980. (Peter Horner)

Trafalgar Square on 4th January 1975. RT 880 carries a 1951 Weymann body and is working from Barking garage on route N95. Some journeys started from Victoria, and worked beyond Barking to Becontree Heath. This bus had been at Barking since January 1973, and had been delicensed a couple of times during its stay there. It was finally withdrawn in June 1975. (Peter Horner)

Route N98 worked from Victoria to Romford, but like many of the night routes few buses worked the whole route. Many started from Trafalgar Square, and worked to Ilford or Chadwell Heath and Seven Kings, as shown here. This journey is starting from Bank, Lombard Street, and RT 3952, working from Barking garage, is fitted with a 1954 Weymann body. The date is 9th October 1976. (Peter Horner)

RTs last worked on route 94 on Saturday 26th August 1978, but RT 422 was suitably decorated on the 25th when this view was taken. Lewisham Bus Station is the venue, and the Park Royal bodied bus is about to start its trip to Orpington. It would be transferred to Barking in the next few days for a couple more years of service, before finishing its life as a trainer at Bexleyheath until withdrawn in 1979. (Peter Horner)

The 700-strong RF class gave good service in the central and country areas since their introduction in 1951. The last to see service in the central area, was RF 507, which worked the 218 into Kingston garage on 30th March 1979. It is shown here on arrival at the garage greeted by a group of enthusiasts. It was delicensed the next day, and sold to a private buyer. (Peter Horner)

It is Sunday 23rd February 1975, and RM 1182 from New Cross is about to leave on the short booked journey of route N82 at 6.26am from Eltham, Yorkshire Grey to Woolwich. The route worked from New Cross to Woolwich, but there were only a few through workings, many turning at Eltham, Well Hall and Lewisham. The route had originally been numbered 182 when introduced after the end of tramway operation on 5/6th July 1952. It was renumbered N82 in June 1968 when the daytime operation of the 182 was withdrawn. (Peter Horner)

A deserted London Bridge Station forecourt on 4th January 1975. RML 2655 from Riverside garage waits for custom on route N89 for the trip to Southall, which is scheduled to take just over an hour. The route was numbered 289 until 1960. The bus carries the body originally fitted to RML 2653, which was new in June 1967. (Peter Horner)

It is 30th September 1984 and RM 1600 from Wood Green has turned short at Trafalgar Square before returning to its home garage. The 29 worked from Victoria to Enfield and (in company with a handful of other day routes) had had extra late journeys from central London dating back to LGOC days. The bus received this body, originally fitted to RM 1763, in December 1980 and it dates from 1963. (Peter Horner)

50

Aldgate terminus on 20th November 1987. It is the last night of Routemasters on route 253, and a decorated bus can be seen in the background with the words 'farewell conductors' on the rear. RM 2131 is working from Ash Grove garage, and carries the 1965 body originally fitted to RM 2190. By this time, RMs carried the operating district logos behind the last lower deck window, and the white roundel on the side. (Peter Horner)

The drab concrete of Stratford bus station is the setting of this January 1981 view. Leyton's RM 1852 waits to depart for Manor House on route 230. D 1164 lurks in the background on circular route S1. The surroundings are stark compared with the bus station of today. (Peter Horner)

Route 187 worked from South Harrow Station to Hampstead Heath, and the latter terminus is depicted here on 26th February 1980. RM 1125 spent three years at Alperton garage, and is ready to depart in this scene. The bus dates from 1962, and although the brake-cooling grilles have been filled in and the centre relief band extended below the ultimate destination, the repositioning of the numberplate has yet to be implemented. (Peter Horner)

A ghostly-looking Whitehall devoid of traffic on 23rd February 1981. RM 533 from Merton garage has a healthy load as it picks up at the stop near Parliament Square. The 77A has travelled from King's Cross, and will make its way south to Raynes Park. The bus carries a 1960 body that was new on RM 404. (Peter Horner)

Mortlake's RM 1192 has worked short to St Paul's, Mansion House, where it rests before returning to base on route 9. The date is Saturday 1st September 1974, and the last journey from here left at 1.28am, arriving back at the garage at 2.10am. (Peter Horner)

The Metrobus was introduced in London in 1978. They were a Metro-Cammell product with a Gardner engine, and were to become a major part of the London fleet throughout the eighties. M 927 was delivered in October 1983, and was a Holloway bus seen working the N100 at the Aldwych on New Year's Day 1993. Due to the celebrations on New Year's Eve, night buses were unable to serve their traditional departure point in Trafalgar Square. In consequence routes were curtailed to start at points around the West End appropriate to their suburban destination. Route N100 operated around the perimeter to link these starting points. Why N100? In those days the internal computer systems couldn't cope with a prefix and a three-digit route number so Chris Holland, who planned the New Year's Eve night network at the time, was confident that N100 would never be used for anything else. Later the systems changed. (Roy Waterhouse)

The Aldwych again on New Year's Day 1993. M 755 was new in February 1982, and is working the N2 to North Finchley from Crystal Palace. Metrobuses shared the bulk of double-deck services with the Leyland Titan during this period. (Roy Waterhouse)

It is October 1989, and Metrobus M 1082, new in 1984, stands at the Edgware terminus of route N5. The route worked to Trafalgar Square and then Aldwych, as in this case, or on some journeys to Victoria. (Roy Waterhouse)

Trafalgar Square on a wet 29th October 1989. T 553 was delivered in August 1982, and had left Willesden Garage on the N6 on its way to Walthamstow Central Station. It seems to be quite busy as it collects people from the rain outside the National Gallery. (Philip Wallis)

In the mid-eighties, 263 Leyland Olympians were delivered and these were the last double deckers to be ordered by London Transport. L 196 was new in November 1986 and takes a break at Victoria Station on route N69 on 20th October 1990. (Roy Waterhouse)

Route NXI worked from Trafalgar Square to Gillingham on Friday and Saturday nights and Saturday and Sunday mornings, with a non-stop section between Strood and Bexley on the return journeys. This Leyland Olympian, L 261, has acquired the registration previously allocated to RM 1002. (Roy Waterhouse)

MTL London route 139 leaves Piccadilly Circus for Trafalgar Square in 1998 before returning to West Hampstead. RM 912 carries the body originally on RM 732, which was built in 1961. It received this on overhaul in 1983. This version of the red livery, where virtually everything was painted red, was considered by many the worst carried by a Routemaster. (Mark Kehoe)

The first batch of RMLs was numbered 880 to 903, and these buses were delivered between July 1961 and January 1962. They were first used on trolleybus replacement route 104 from Finchley. On overhaul, the bodies stayed within the batch and not transferred to later production buses. RML 884 waits at Victoria Station on route 38 with the rather ugly camera between decks on display. The body dates from November 1961 when it was fitted to RML 896. The date is 14th April 2005. (Phil Halewood)

Looking rather tired and weary, RML 892 works the 159, which was destined to be the last route of all to operate the type, the last day being 9th December 2005. The bus carries a body built in October 1961 that, when new, was fitted to RML 888. This view was taken in October 2005 in Regent Street. (Phil Halewood)

Two Routemasters passing Trafalgar Square with Canada House behind. RM 1312 on the left has been re-registered and is on the 159 passing RM 1204 on the 9. RM 1312 is now with an owner in Holland. (Mark Kehoe)

Flat-fare 513 was a Monday-Friday route from London Bridge Station to Waterloo. MBA 569 was a 1969 AEC Merlin with MCW bodywork and operated from Victoria (Gillingham Street) garage. It carries a black blind instead of the usual blue carried by Red Arrow routes, and is seen at London Bridge. (Peter Horner)

The London General Omnibus Company opened Plumstead bus garage in 1913. DM 1059 from New Cross leaves for Camden Town on 25th October 1981. The 53 terminated at Plumstead Common on Mondays to Saturdays, but was extended here on Sundays. This was the last day it turned here, as the garage closed the following Friday. The bus has a Park Royal body, and was delivered in 1975. (Peter Horner)

The MD class consisted of 164 Metropolitan buses with MCW bodywork and Scania running units. MD 32 from Peckham garage is seen here on route N85 at the Embankment terminus on 23rd October 1981. Route 285 replaced all-night tram 5 on the night of 6/7th January 1952, and it was renumbered N85 in October 1960. (Peter Horner)

Scania Metropolitan MD 111 was the last bus on route 192 to enter Plumstead (AM) garage in the early hours of 31st October 1981. The garage closed that night and operations were transferred to the new garage coded PD. The bus is waiting at Lewisham Bus Station ready for its next trip to Woodlands Estate and home garage. (Peter Horner)

The T-class Leyland Titan commenced delivery in August 1978 and continued until the end of 1984. T 881 from Bromley is seen here on route 161 at Woolwich, Monk Street in March 1994. These buses, together with the Metrobus, became the major part of the double-deck London fleet during this period. (Peter Horner)

Route B16 served the Ferrier Estate at Kidbrooke, and links it with the shopping areas at Eltham and Bexleyheath. London Central DML 17 picks up at Eltham Church on 12th December 2006 and the driver takes refreshment while the passengers all try to find a place on the already crowded bus. The bus is a Dennis Dart with Marshall body built in 1999. The run-down Ferrier Estate was demolished in 2015/2016 to make way for more upmarket flats. (John King)

Paddington on 28th January 2005. VNL 32270 in the First fleet is a Volvo B7TL / Transbus ALX400 which was new in 2003. Route 23 is a 24-hour service on its way to Ladbroke Grove. (Philip Wallis)

Blackfriars Bridge on 13th December 2014. The lit dome of St Paul's looks down on the scene as London General Dennis Dart SLF / Plaxton Pointer 2 No.8308 picks up a passenger on route 100 bound for the Elephant and Castle. The bus was new in 2004. In the background is the new Blackfriars Station, the only station to have entrances on both sides of the Thames. (Jason Cross)

CT Plus HTL 9 is collecting a passenger at the stop at Norton Folgate on its way to Hackney Wick on route 388 on 6th April 2006. The bus is a Dennis Trident / East Lancs Lolyne delivered in 2003. The route is operated out of TfL-owned Ash Grove garage, which is shared with Arriva. (John King)

Abellio 9034 is a 2005 Volvo B7TL / Wrightbus Eclipse Gemini. It is at the Elephant and Castle loading on the 343 to New Cross Gate on 7th November 2014. To the right of the bus can be seen the 'Elephant & Castle' statue which originally adorned the pub of the same name slightly further north on the corner of New Kent Road and Newington Butts. (Rob Telford)

The articulated or 'bendy' buses, as they became known, first worked Red Arrow routes in London in June 2002. In February the following year they started work on the 436, and many other routes soon followed. Mercedes-Benz Citaro MA 91 in the Arriva fleet is seen in Bishopsgate in 2006. (Philip Wallis)

The elegant design of Cockfosters station graces the background in this January 2011 view. The Piccadilly Line opened to here at the end of July 1933. Metroline DES 795 waits for passengers before departure. It is a 2007 Enviro200. (John King)

An Underground strike on 9th January 2017 was one of a number of similar occasions when many extra buses were drafted in to help. This ex-Arriva 2004 VDL DB250RS(LF) / Wrightbus Gemini from the Kent operator Chalkwell was one of them. It is seen here at Aldgate East working the 25 to Holborn. (Lgee Faure)

Another vehicle drafted in to help with the Underground strike extras on 9th January 2017 was this Essex-based Trustybus Scania Omnicity. It is at rest between trips on the 108 and is pictured at Stratford International. The bus had been new to Metrobus. (Lgee Faure)

TN 1332 in the First fleet is a Transbus Trident / President delivered in May 2003. It is about to depart from Uxbridge Station on the A10 for Heathrow Airport on 19th September 2004. The last section of this route between Stockley Business Park and Heathrow, was non-stop.

On a cold and wet night on 12th January 2015, Go-Ahead No.937 is at Lewisham Station. It is a busy point with connections to the Docklands Light railway. The bus is an East Lancs-bodied Scania Omnidekka, and is operating an additional service from London Bridge to Lewisham (in one direction) to provide support to the 21 during one of the stages of the rebuilding of London Bridge station. It is operated by Metrobus (the normal 21 is London Central) and will return empty either back to London Bridge or possibly to its garage depending on the time.. (Lgee Faure)

Arriva VLW 184 pauses at the stop opposite St Clement Dane's in the Strand on 10th November 2009 on route 76. It has travelled down from Tottenham, and will shortly cross Waterloo Bridge. The bus is a Volvo B7TL / Wright Eclipse Gemini built in 2003. (John King)

The 85 is a 24-hour route between Kingston and Putney Bridge Station. This view is in Eden Street, Kingston on 25th October 2015. Go-Ahead WVL 21 is a 2002 Volvo B7TL / Wright Eclipse Gemini. (Lgee Faure)

Transdev VH 16 on route 13 in the Strand on 27th March 2014 is a Volvo B5LH / Wrightbus Gemini 2 new the previous year. The bus is operated by the London Sovereign subsidiary of Transdev. (Rob Telford)

Tower Transit VNW 32372 is a Volvo B7TL / Wrightbus Eclipse Gemini built in 2004. The N31 works from Camden Town to Clapham Junction, and waits here at Earl's Court in April 2017, in the deserted street which is spied on from a rather sinister-looking camera high above the road behind the bus. (Jason Cross)

The scene is Thomas Street in Woolwich on 3rd February 2010. Route 51, long associated with this area, will make its way through Plumstead Common, Welling, Blackfen and Sidcup before reaching Orpington. The bus is a Scania Omnicity, new in 2009, and is numbered 15077 in the Selkent fleet. (John King)

On 12th December 2015, Arriva Wrightbus Gemini 2 DW 283 is at the Trafalgar Square stop on the 159. The Marble Arch to Streatham service is a 24-hour route, and was the last to see regular Routemaster operation. The bus was built in 2010. (Lgee Faure)

The E8 works from Ealing Broadway, seen here, to Brentford. On 25th February 2016, Metroline MM 785, a 2007 MAN 12.240 / MCV Evolution bus, leaves the terminus. (Lgee Faure)

It is a snowy night on 2nd December 2010 in Erith. Selkent Optare Versa 37004 is waiting to leave for Queen Elizabeth Hospital on route 469. It is a 2009 delivery and is working from Plumstead garage. (Justin Bailey)

It is the Charing Cross end of the Strand on 18th May 2015. Go-Ahead WVL 473 works the N44 to Sutton. The route is an extension of the day route 44 beyond Tooting. The bus is a Volvo B9TL / Wrightbus Eclipse Gemini 2 built in 2012. (Lgee Faure)

This is St John's Road, Clapham Junction a few days before Christmas 2015. London Central WVL 304 is on the 24-hour route 37 from Peckham and is a Volvo B9TL / Wrightbus Eclipse Gemini 2 built in 2009. (Lgee Faure)

The 207 has its origins in the trolleybus route 607, which it replaced in 1960. The daytime route works from Hayes By Pass to White City, but the night version runs on to Holborn. Metroline SN 1927, which should be displaying N207, is a Scania Omnicity built in 2011, and is at Ealing Broadway on 15th February 2015. (Lgee Faure)

Tottenham Court Road in July 2016. A convoy of buses makes its way north. Metroline VW 1264, a 2009 Wrightbus Gemini 2-bodied Volvo B9TL, starts its journey to North Finchley, followed by TE 886, a 2008 Enviro400 on the N5 to Edgware. Bringing up the rear is LT 533, a 2015 New Routemaster on the 73. (Lgee Faure)

It is Saturday 27th December 2014 in Oxford Street, and with Christmas over the crowds persist as the sales are now on. Tower Transit DN 33786 is on the 23 bound for Westbourne Park. The bus is a 2012 ADL E40D. LT 342 on the 137 is on the left. (Jason Cross)

Oxford Street on 26th November 2016, and Christmas decorations abound in this view on the run-up to the holiday. From left to right are Metroline VWH 2022, a Volvo B5LH / Wrightbus Gemini 2 from 2014, London United VH 45190, a Volvo B5LH / Wrightbus Gemini 3 new in 2016, and London United ADH 18, a 2010 Enviro400. (Justin Bailey)

The 288 is a short route from Queensbury to Broadfields Estate. Arriva DWL 91, a 2006 VDL/DAF Wrightbus Cadet, is waiting at Edgware in April 2016. (Lgee Faure)

The bus station at Edmonton Green in November 2014. The 259 is still based on the old trolleybus 659 and tram 59 before it, working south to King's Cross. (Lgee Faure)

WVL 164 travels up Shaftesbury Avenue in the heart of Soho on a balmy August evening in 2013. Route 14 has served this street for over 100 years and is today one of London's many 24-hour bus services. If Crossrail 2 goes ahead there will be an entrance to its Tottenham Court Road station just behind the photographer of this view. (Piero Cruciatti)

Bromley South on 4th November 2017. Bromley garage's 19135 hasn't far to go before turning at Bromley North for its return trip to Chislehurst. The bus is a 2006 ADL Enviro400, and waits at one of the many stops in London now lit by a solar-powered lamp on each side. (Capital Transport)

London Bridge Station in the shadow of the new development there. Go-Ahead Mercedes-Benz Citaro MEC 6 dates from 2009 and waits to leave on the 521 for Waterloo. It will get to Waterloo via Cannon Street, St Paul's and Holborn. (Rob Telford)

After much hype, the first 'New Bus for London' appeared in 2012. It was certainly a very new and very fresh design, and unlike anything else on the road. LT 580 was delivered in 2015, and is seen at the Brantwood Road stop in Tottenham working the 149. (Peter Horrex)

This rear offside view of LT 738 opposite Waterloo station shows the effect of the two glazed staircases at night. This stretch of Waterloo Road has four LT-operated services along it and also has Boris Bus-lookalike Enviro400 Citys on the 26. (Capital Transport)

Two Boris Buses have just entered the Strand from Trafalgar Square on 6th December 2015. LT 49, built in 2013, is followed by 2015 delivery LT 481, as they make their way to Liverpool Street on the 11, as buses had done on this route for over a hundred years. (Jason Cross)

Metroline BYD 1473 has been in service for two days at the time of this photo. It is a BYD K8SR electric bus. The N98 is an extension of the daytime 98 from Willesden Garage to Stanmore, but this journey is being curtailed at the garage. The date is 7th May 2016. (Lgee Faure)

The 243 still travels the same route as its predecessor, trolleybus 543/643, which it replaced in July 1961, apart from the southerly extension to Waterloo, where this shot was taken on 11th March 2017. This Volvo B5LH / Wrightbus Gemini 3 is HV 224 in the Arriva fleet, and had just been delivered. (Phil Halewood)

Wellesley Road, Croydon in February 2016. A row of three buses wait at this busy point, which is also on the Tramlink network. The centre vehicle is Arriva T 137, a 2010 Enviro400, on route 250. The Whitgift Shopping Centre is here, and to the south are the large Fairfield Halls. (Lgee Faure)

Arriva route 78 at Liverpool Street on 28th December 2015. HA 4 is an ADL Enviro400H City that was delivered in 2015. The bus has travelled from Shoreditch and will shortly cross Tower Bridge on its way to Bermondsey and Nunhead. (Phil Halewood)

Finsbury Park in November 2011. Arriva DW 496 is a Wrightbus Gemini 2 integral built that year. It is setting off for Warren Street on route 29, and has so far managed to escape having adverts posted on its side. (Peter Horrex)

Waiting at the lights at Wood Green in November 2011, on the left is Arriva DW 468, a new Wrightbus Gemini 2 vehicle, alongside fellow fleet member ENL 44, an Enviro200 new in 2009. The 29 will soon terminate but the 184 will continue through Bounds Green and Arnos Grove on its way to Barnet. (Peter Horrex)

The 24-hour 134 route starts its journey here at Tottenham Court Road travelling north to North Finchley. Metroline VPL 138 is a Volvo B7TL / Plaxton President built in 2001, seen here in November 2008. (Peter Horrex)

The Jubilee Line to Stratford created a newly served area at North Greenwich when it opened here in May 1999. The Millennium Dome nearby became an attraction, and the station soon became busy with commuters too. In April 2011, London Central WVL 359 loads up on the 422. It is a 2010 Volvo B9TL / Wrightbus Gemini 2. (John King)

Route 279 still runs part of what was trolleybus route 679 and tram 79 before it. This is Ponders End on 30th October 2014, and Arriva T 259 has travelled down from Waltham Cross. It is an ADL Enviro400, new in 2012. (Peter Horrex)

Working the RVI from Covent Garden to Tower Gateway is First Bus WSH 62991. It is a hydrogen fuel-cell bus new in 2010 and is a VDL SB200 with Wrightbus Pulsar 2 body. The bus is shown at Aldwych, turning into Strand before crossing Waterloo Bridge. (Rob Telford)

Stagecoach 15043 is a Scania Omnicity which was delivered in 2009. It is pictured at Chingford at the start of its trip south on the 97 to Stratford City. It will follow what was former trolleybus route 697 for most of the way, although this was not the service that originally replaced it back in 1960. The date is November 2017. (Peter Horrex)

Sullivan Buses operate route 217, and brand new E 75, an Enviro400 MMC, is leaving Turnpike Lane Station on 22nd November 2017 for a trip along the main Cambridge Road to Waltham Cross. (Peter Horrex)

London United ADH45014 was originally numbered ADH 14 and is an ADL Enviro400 delivered in 2010. The Regent Street Christmas lights are on in this November 2017 view, as the vehicle ends its journey on the 94 for return to Acton Green. (Capital Transport)

Shaftesbury Avenue is part of Theatreland, and this November 2017 view shows Arriva 24-hour route 19 from Finsbury Park to Battersea Bridge. The bus is a Volvo B5LH / Wrightbus Gemini 3 delivered in 2017, and numbered HV 376 in the fleet. (Capital Transport)

Local route 379 connects Yardley Estate with Turnpike Lane Station, seen here on 23rd November 2017. The bus is London General WS 80, which is a Wrightbus Streetlite WF delivered earlier in the year. (Peter Horrex)

Piccadilly Circus in November 2017. The 14 is one of many former cross-London routes to have been curtailed in the centre in more recent years. Running from Putney Heath to Warren Street now, instead of the previous routeing on to Hornsey Rise, London General MHV 88 is a new MCV EvoSeti-bodied Volvo B5LH. (Capital Transport)

New developments were added above and to the left and right of the Underground Station at Morden, which give it the appearance it has today. It opened in September 1926, and was a stand-alone building at that time. On route 164 is Go Ahead SE 280, an ADL E20D/Enviro200 new in 2015. (Rob Telford)